# Contents

# Introduction

It is impossible to *start* a family ministry. Why? Because every church—your church—is *already* ministering to families. You can expand that ministry, you can improve it, you can meet more family needs, but your ministry to families began when your church was formed.

A family ministry is not something you add to your regular church program. It is integrated throughout all your ministries.

• Sermons and Bible teaching programs help people grow in their relationship with Christ. As a result family members are better equipped for handling relationships within the home.

• When a couple receives premarital counseling from a member of the church staff that is ministering to families.

• When you share a book on family living with parents or add a family life book to your church library you are ministering to families.

• When you add a family life elective to the Sunday School courses—that is a family ministry.

• When you give a word of encouragement or advice to a young couple who are worrying about their first child—that is a family ministry.

• When you help a widow, accept and care about a divorced person, or spend time with someone who is elderly and lonely you are ministering to families.

• Yes, a family life ministry is more than programs and events that focus on family life. It is a church lifestyle in which individuals are equipped and encouraged to live in harmony together in their homes. It is also church leaders modeling with their own families, the principles that help build successful Christian homes.

Family ministry is basic in God's Word and in His church. God created the first family—Adam and Eve. God was the first family minister as He instructed Adam and Eve how they should live on earth. And God's instruction to families did not end with Adam and Eve. Woven throughout the Bible are threads of teaching on family living—basics of healthy family life—that form the pattern for successful Christian families.

### Following the Thread

In the Old Testament, family living is defined: God builds the family (see Ps. 127); husbands and wives are to become one (see Gen. 2:24); parents are to teach godly values to their children (see Deut. 6:4-9) and to discipline them (see Prov. 19:18); children are to obey and honor their parents (see Prov. 1:8, Exod. 20:12).

The thread continues throughout the New Testament. Husbands are to love their wives (see Col. 3:19); the oneness of husband and wife is reemphasized (see Eph. 5:21-33). Children are to be brought up in the discipline and instruction of the Lord (see Eph. 6:4).

6

Children are to obey their parents (see Eph. 6:1-3).

The New Testament stresses the importance of godly family living in a new way. A primary qualification for elder and deacon within the church family is that they manage their own households well (see 1 Tim. 3:4,12).

Dr. Gene Getz in his book, *The Measure of a Family*, points out that relatively few New Testament Scriptures make a direct reference to family life. In Ephesians only 16 out of 155 verses are specifically family directed. Six of Paul's letters make no direct reference to the family; only four of his other letters contain brief material. Hebrews, James, Jude, John's epistles and Revelation make no specific comments on the family. Peter, in his first epistle, speaks about the family but says nothing in his second letter.[1] However, even though the Scriptures only briefly outline principles of family living, according to Dr. Getz, many Scriptures that were directed to the church family also apply to the home. In the early stages of Christianity, the home was the church (see 1 Cor. 16:15).

Dr. Getz draws an important conclusion from these observations:

> *What was written to the Church was also written to individual families. Most of the New Testament, then, can be applied directly to individual family units. We do have a guidebook for the family unit! The Church simply becomes an umbrella concept that includes the home. The family is really the Church in miniature. True, on occasions, the New Testament writers zero in on special needs that are uniquely related to family living. But in the most part, what was written to believers as a whole applies directly to Christian living in the smaller context of the home.*[2]

7

### The Church and the Family

A Scripture passage that is written specifically to the church but has important implications for the family and a family ministry is Ephesians 4:11-16. In these verses the church leaders are instructed to equip believers for ministry:

> *And He gave some as apostles, and some as prophets, and some as evangelists, and some as pastors and teachers, for the equipping of the saints for the work of service, to the building up of the body of Christ; until we all attain to the unity of the faith, and of the knowledge of the Son of God, to a mature man, to the measure of the stature which belongs to the fulness of Christ. As a result, we are no longer to be children, tossed here and there by waves, and carried about by every wind of doctrine, by the trickery of men, by craftiness in deceitful scheming; but speaking the truth in love, we are to grow up in all aspects unto Him, who is the head, even Christ, from whom the whole body, being fitted and held together by that which every joint supplies, according to the proper working of each individual part, causes the growth of the body for the building up of itself in love.*

Paul tells the church that leaders are to equip the saints for "work of service." This work of service, or ministry, is the building up of the Body of Christ—the church—with the ultimate goal being to help each person become mature in Christ—the Head. The Body of Christ then grows properly in love because each part is functioning properly in love.

The implications for a family ministry are obvious. The "church in miniature," the family, also grows properly when each part is functioning properly in love. If each part is not functioning properly within the home the church is affected. For the church is comprised mainly of families.

Parents are responsible for building up the Body of Christ in their own homes. It is in the home that loving relationships are taught. The churches are responsible for equipping parents for their primary ministry of teaching loving relationships at home.

The purpose of this book, then, is not to help you— the church leader—"to start a family ministry." It is to help you evaluate your ministry to families and plan to meet an even greater amount of needs. This book should help you see what you are currently doing and guide you into expanding the horizons of your church's family ministries.

The success of your ministry to families is not based upon how large your church is or how many "outstanding family ideas" you can have in a year. Success is measured by how well you are equipping families, in a steady, determined manner, to (1) *grow closer in their relationship with Christ* and (2) *in their relationships with one another within the home.* If you can look back each year and see measurable growth in these two areas, then you have a successful family ministry.

## Formula for Planning an Effective Family Ministry

I find that virtually all family needs can be grouped into five major areas:

- A personal relationship with God
- Husband-wife relationships
- Family relationships
- Family teaching
- Family in ministry

From these five areas of family needs come the purposes and goals for an effective family ministry. How this works is what this book is all about.

Study the following diagram and terms. These concepts are the base of my formula for planning an ongoing ministry to families in the church.

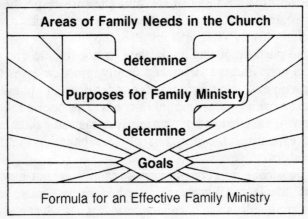

**Areas of Family Needs in the Church**

determine

**Purposes for Family Ministry**

determine

**Goals**

Formula for an Effective Family Ministry

## An Explanation of Terms

*Areas of Family Need.* In this book we define five major areas of family needs. These definitions are five general statements concerning areas of need that church leaders need to consider as they plan for ministering to the needs of families in the congregation. I've listed these areas of family need already. Here's the list again: (1) a personal relationship with God; (2) husband-wife relationships; (3) family relationships; (4) family teaching; (5) family in ministry.

*Purposes.* After you—the church leader—have identified the areas of greatest family needs in your church you are ready to establish purposes for your family ministry based on the needs of your congregation. Exactly what is a purpose? A purpose states a direction you want your family ministry to take, something you want to achieve.[3] When your purposes have been established you are ready to set your goals.

*Goals.* What is a goal? According to Edward R. Dayton and Ted W. Engstrom in their book, *Strategy for Living*, "A goal is a plan for a future event which you believe is both accomplishable and measurable. Measurable in terms of what is to be done and how long it takes to do it."[4]

## Reflect and Respond Section

To help you and your church staff form a philosophy for your ministry to families, to help you determine areas of family need and to plan ways to meet those needs, I have included "Reflect and Respond" sections throughout this book.

You may "reflect and respond" to the questions and statements individually or as a group. I feel that the best way to use this book is for your church leaders, the family life committee or Christian education committee to go through it together, discussing the "Reflect and Respond" sections in depth.

## Reflect and Respond

1. Using the information in the final paragraphs of the introduction write (in your own words) definitions for the following terms as they relate to family ministry in the church:

Areas of Family Need—


Purposes of Family Ministry—


Goals for Family Ministry—

2. List ways your church is ministering to families.

3. In the opinion of Dr. Gene Getz and the author of this book, the family is the church in miniature. Do you agree or disagree? If this statement is true, what implications does it have for your church? Your church families?

4. List the five basic areas of family needs. Which of the five areas touch on needs you are aware of in your church?

5. The author states that in an effective family life ministry, the church leaders model, with their own families, the principles that build strong Christian families. In a time of silence, identify at least one way you want to improve your family's modeling of a Christian lifestyle. Ask God for direction and strength.

---

**Notes**

1. Gene Getz, *The Measure of a Family* (Glendale, CA: Regal Books, 1973), p. 13.
2. *The Measure of a Family*, p. 13.
3. Edward R. Dayton and Ted W. Engstrom, *Strategy for Living* (Glendale, CA: Regal Books, 1976), p. 49.
4. *Strategy for Living*, p. 49.

# 1
# A Biblical Base
# for Family
# Ministry

Any church ministry to families must have a biblical basis. The church leader involved in family ministry must know: What does God's Word teach about the family? What is God's ideal for families?

We will ask these questions about each of the basic five areas of family needs as we think through biblical reasons for family ministry in the church.

## Area 1—A Personal Relationship with God

Man's first relationship was with God. Adam was created by God for fellowship with Him—a personal relationship. This relationship has always remained primary with God. God's plan, however, included other relationships for man. God created the first family relationship, Eve for Adam. The deepest of human relationships resulted—marriage.

13

But with the first human relationship came tragedy. The Fall. Adam and Eve sinned, eating of the forbidden fruit. Their perfect relationship with God was broken. The remainder of the Old Testament is the story of that broken relationship between man and God, and God's plan to restore that relationship through His Son. God worked His plan through the nation of Israel. And "when the time had fully come" God sent His own Son to restore the personal relationship between Himself and man (Gal. 4:4, *RSV*).

It is this restored relationship with God through Jesus Christ that is the basis of all family living. Second Corinthians 5:17,18 puts it so beautifully: "Therefore if any man is in Christ, he is a new creature; the old things passed away; behold, new things have come. Now all these things are from God, who reconciled us to Himself through Christ and gave us the ministry of reconciliation."

This Scripture portion speaks of the new birth and the new life that is a result of a personal relationship with God. When a person is reborn and steps into the new life, he is motivated and empowered by God to become a loving person—a loving family member.

The new birth does not mean instant maturity, however. A family member does not have perfect loving relationships with all others in his family the moment he is reborn. There is that process of growing and struggling that occurs in all new life before full potential and beauty is achieved. It is this growth of which Ephesians 4:15 speaks when Paul says, "We are to grow up in all aspects into Him, who is the head, even Christ."

God has not left us alone in our struggle. He gives us His Spirit at the moment of our new birth. This Holy Spirit gives us the strength to grow. Ephesians 3:14-19 says:

*For this reason, I bow my knees before the Father, from whom every family in heaven and on earth derives its name, that He would grant you, according to the riches of His glory, to be strengthened with power through His Spirit in the inner man; so that Christ may dwell in your hearts through faith; and that you, being rooted and grounded in love, may be able to comprehend with all the saints what is the breadth and length and height and depth, and to know the love of Christ which surpasses knowledge, that you may be filled up to all the fulness of God.*

Family members must first have a growing relationship with Christ to have a growing relationship with one another. To minister to families the church must first help them grow in their personal relationship with God. To grow one must have food. God's food for spiritual growth in His Word.

*All scripture is inspired by God and is useful for teaching the faith and correcting error, for resetting the direction of a man's life and training him in good living. The scriptures are the comprehensive equipment of the man of God, and fit him fully for all branches of his work (2 Tim. 3:16,17 Phillips).*

A strong Bible teaching ministry, then, is essential to a successful ministry to families. A Bible teaching program that enables families to grow toward maturity in Christ is vital. All other relationships of life are dependent upon God's ideal—a close personal relationship with Him through Jesus Christ.

## Reflect and Respond

1. The author states that the first purpose of a family

ministry is to provide a strong Bible teaching ministry that will help individuals grow in their personal relationship with God. Do you agree or disagree? Give a reason for your answer.

2. In what ways will a close personal relationship with God affect:
a. husband-wife relationships?
b. family relationships (communication, discipline, etc.)?
c. family teaching (teaching biblical truths to your children)?
d. family in ministry (service both inside and outside the church)?

3. On a scale of 1 (the lowest) to 10 (the highest), rank your church's effectiveness in helping people grow in their personal relationship with God.

4. In what ways do you feel that your church can improve its effectiveness in helping people grow in their personal relationship with God?

5. Are leaders in your church modeling a close personal relationship with God?

**Area 2—Husband-Wife Relationships**
The second purpose of a family ministry is to help build strong and happy marriages. Next to nurturing the individual family member's relationship to God, this is

the most vital area of the church's ministry to families.

God first created man for fellowship with Himself. But God also wanted man to have a deep human relationship so He created Eve for Adam. Thus the first human relationship was formed—marriage. God's ideal was for marriage to be broken only by death. As Jesus explained in Mark 10:6-9: "From the beginning of creation, God made them male and female. For this cause a man shall leave his father and mother, and the two shall become one flesh; consequently they are no longer two, but one flesh. What therefore God has joined together, let no man separate."

God's ideal for marriage remains unchanged today. *It is the teaching responsibility of the church to enable husbands and wives to discover biblical principles that will help them build strong and lasting marriages.* Other family relationships are heavily dependent upon the quality of the husband-wife relationship.

Biblically successful marriages happen when couples understand God's specific instructions on marriage, as well as His teachings related to loving human relationships, and apply them to their own lives. Teachings on marriage can be grouped into three major areas.

*The uniqueness and permanence of marriage.* Genesis 2:18-25 gives us a beautiful account of the uniqueness and permanence of marriage. God created Adam and all the animals but still saw Adam as being incomplete. "Then the Lord God said, 'It is not good for the man to be alone; I will make him a helper suitable for him'" (Gen. 2:18).

Even though Adam had a perfect, personal relationship with God there was still something missing—a human relationship of the most intimate nature. Adam needed fellowship with another human, so God filled this need. God caused a deep sleep to come upon Adam

17

and created from his rib the helper he needed to make his life complete. "And the Lord God fashioned into a woman the rib which He had taken from the man, and brought her to the man" (Gen. 2:22). God's crown of creation is now complete. He has created man and woman in His own image for fellowship with Himself and each other. This is the uniqueness of marriage.

Since marriage is created by God, by its very nature it is to be a permanent relationship. "And the man said, 'This is now bone of my bones, and flesh of my flesh; she shall be called Woman, because she was taken out of Man.' For this cause a man shall leave his father and his mother, and shall cleave to his wife; and they shall become one flesh" (Gen. 2:23,24).

There are three important elements in verse 24: *leave*, *cleave*, and *one flesh*. To leave means to break the ties of dependence to one's own family. Cleave implies sticking to something like glue. It denotes permanence. This permanence comes from God—He supplies the glue. "Consequently they are no more two, but one flesh. What therefore *God has joined together*, let no man separate" (Matt. 19:6, italics added).

When God joins a couple together in marriage they are no longer two people. They become one. They belong to one another. God pronounces an immediate oneness, "they . . . become one flesh." And they continue to grow into becoming one flesh as they submit themselves to one another, meeting one another's needs. According to Jesus the only thing that breaks that oneness is adultery.

Paul and Peter both said that believers should stay with their unbelieving spouses whereby the unbelievers may be saved (see 1 Cor. 7:12-16; 1 Pet. 3:1-7).

*Roles of love in marriage.* Growing in oneness should be a goal of all marriages. An integral part of this growth is a proper understanding and application of husband and wife roles. In Ephesians 5:21-35 Paul describes the proper roles husbands and wives are to have.

Husbands and wives are to be subject to one another. "And be subject to one another in the fear of Christ." (Eph. 5:21). What a way to start teaching about husband and wife roles! In Christ we are all spiritually equal. As spiritual equals, no matter what our status or role, we are to submit our own desires to that of others. We are to think of others' needs first—our own needs last!

The wife is to be the follower-lover. Verses 22 and 24 go on to say that wives specifically are to be in subjection to their husbands. That is, they are to submit to the leadership of their husbands in the same way they submit to the leadership of the Lord. As the church is subject to Christ so is the wife to be subject to her husband. With this subjection should go love and respect (see v. 33).

The home needs proper leadership to become all God wants it to be. God has designated man to be that leader (see 1 Cor. 7:3,4), not because he is more qualified or superior spiritually to woman, but because God said, "I want man to be the leader." The husband, however, is to be a certain kind of leader. "For the husband is the head of the wife, as Christ also is the head of the church, He Himself being the Savior of the body" (Eph. 5:23).

The husband is to pattern his leadership after Christ's leadership to the church. What an example! For Jesus was a *servant leader* to the church, finally giving His life for it. Philippians 2:1-11 pictures Christ's leadership so beautifully—a vivid description of servant leadership. Christ emptied Himself, took the form of a servant, humbled Himself, and became obedient, even unto death (see Phil. 2:7,8).

What wife couldn't submit herself to this type of leadership? A husband who is serving her and the family—more concerned about their needs than his own—living with his wife in an understanding way (see 1 Pet. 3:7).

*Sex in marriage.* Sex in the Bible has two purposes. The first is to enrich the marriage relationship, "And they became one flesh" (see Gen. 2:24). The second is for procreation, "Be fruitful and multiply" (Gen. 1:22). Paul says in 1 Corinthians 7:3,4 that husband and wife are to meet one another's needs for sex in a marriage relationship. But sex outside of marriage, adultery, is forbidden by God. "You shall not commit adultery" (Exod. 20:14).

Woven intricately into these three areas of marriage —uniqueness and permanency, roles of love, and sex— are principles of communication. God's specific instructions on marriage and communication, if lived out, will result in growing Christian marriages.

**Reflect and Respond**

1. The author lists husband-wife relationships as the second most important goal of a family ministry. Do you agree or disagree? Why?

2. In what specific ways does the husband-wife relationship affect other relationships within the home?

3. What are some of your thoughts on the following? The uniqueness and permanence of marriage:

Role of love in marriage:

Sex in marriage:

4. In what specific ways have you observed husband-wife roles affecting the growth of a marriage relationship? Making marriage stronger? Weakening a marriage?

5. Evaluate the quality of the marriages in your church:
What percentage of them are poor? _____percent.
What percentage of them are fair? _____percent.
What percentage of them are good? _____percent.
What percentage of them are excellent?_____percent.
    The total should equal        100 percent.

6. Is your marriage a model for other couples? Are the marriages of leaders in your church models for other couples?

### Area 3—Family Relationships

This third purpose is a large one. It includes the many family relationships that occur within the larger family of God—the church—as well as within the home.

*Parent-child relationships.* God's Word does not give a manual on child rearing but it does give some general principles on discipline. In Hebrews 12:7 the writer uses the analogy of father-son discipline to show why God disciplines us. Discipline, says the writer, shows love: "For the Lord disciplines him whom he loves" (Heb. 12:6, *RSV*). Even though we do not find this pleasant at the time, the end result is for our benefit. "Later it yields the peaceful fruit of righteousness to those who have been trained by it" (Heb. 12:11, *RSV*). An ideal parent disciplines in love.

The word discipline comes from the root word disciple. To disciple suggests a positive teaching approach to discipline. While God does not outline a comprehensive list of methods of discipline (except for the "rod" in Prov. 13:24), He does tell us the spirit in which we should discipline our children—discipline should focus on encouragement rather than discouragement. Paul, in Ephesians 6:4, says, "Fathers, do not provoke your children to anger; but bring them up in the discipline and instruction of the Lord." In Colossians 3:21, Paul suggests that harsh discipline will "discourage" children *(RSV)*. And in 1 Thessalonians 2:11 we read, "For you know how, like a father with his children, we exhorted each one of you and encouraged you and charged you." In these verses we see the ideal of a Christian father who takes time to personally encourage his children with loving, consistent discipline.

Parents are to teach their children a productive Christian life-style. Proverbs 22:6 says, "Train up a child in the way he should go, even when he is old he will not depart from it." The primary meaning of this verse is that children should be given instruction based upon their level of maturity. What instruction? This verse does not say, but from the content of the entire book of Proverbs we can assume that this includes all of life—communication, how to treat your neighbor, acceptance of correction, sex education, how to choose friends, diligence, self-esteem, work, study habits, etc. But these things should be taught at proper times, when the child is psychologically and spiritually ready for them.

*Children-parent relationships.* There are only a few Scriptures that tell specific relationships children are to have with their parents. Children are to honor their parents: "Honor your father and your mother" (Exod. 20:12). Paul put honor and obedience together in his instructions to children in Ephesians 6:1,2: "Children, obey your parents in the Lord, for this is right. Honor your father and mother." Paul, writing to the Colossians, tells children to obey their parents "for this is well-pleasing to the Lord" (Col. 3:20).

Proverbs 1:8 tells children to listen to their parents' teaching: "Hear, my son, your father's instruction, and do not forsake your mother's teaching." Correction from parents is to be valued by children: "A wise son accepts his father's discipline, but a scoffer does not listen to rebuke" (Prov. 13:1).

*Family communication.* Since the home is the church of God in miniature, the many Scriptures that deal with communication between the church members apply as well to the family members in the home. Philippians 2:1-11 is a foundation for all family communication. Verses 3 and 4 capture the spirit of this communication: "Do nothing from selfishness or empty conceit, but with humility of mind let each of you regard one another as more important than himself; do not merely look for your own personal interests, but also for the interests of others." Verses 5 through 11 show how Christ is an example of these principles.

The goal of family communication should be to follow the loving example of Christ. Jesus spent time communicating with persons individually as well as groups of people. The family must spend quality time together, talking, listening, understanding, if loving communication is to happen.

*Single adults.* There are two classifications of single adults, the formerly married and the unmarried. The formerly married consists of two groups, the widowed and the divorced or separated. Scriptures show a great concern for widows. If possible widows were to be cared for by their own families. "Real widows" *(RSV)*, those who were alone, who had no one to take care of them were to be cared for by the church (see 1 Tim. 5:3-16).

The church then becomes the family of real widows.

The church is also responsible to love and encourage those who are single through divorce or separation. Many of these single persons, especially women, are also parents. The church can be an extended family to these families.

Jesus had very little to say about those who never married. In Matthew 19:12 He speaks about eunuchs "who have been so from birth, . . . eunuchs who have been made eunuchs by men, and . . . eunuchs who have made themselves eunuchs for the sake of the kingdom of heaven" *(RSV)*. In this last phrase He is referring to the person who has chosen to remain single for the sake of the work of the Kingdom of God.

The apostle Paul indicated this same idea when he said, "I wish that all men were even as I myself am. However, each man has his own gift from God, one in this manner, and another in that. But I say to the unmarried and to widows that it is good for them if they remain even as I" (1 Cor. 7:7,8). Paul, like Jesus, sees singleness as a gift from God.

*The aging.* Another neglected part of the family of God has been the elderly. God, however, has always valued older people's contribution to His world. Old age brought with it wisdom, "Wisdom is with the aged, and understanding in length of days" (Job 12:12, *RSV*). If King Rehoboam had listened to the counsel of the older men, "the old men, who had stood before Solomon his father" (1 Kings 12:6, *RSV*), he would not have lost half his kingdom. The young king, instead, listened to his young friends and the result was that his kingdom was divided.

Old age is honored. Leviticus 19:32 says, "You shall rise up before the hoary head, and honor the face of an old man, and you shall fear your God: I am the Lord"

*(RSV)*. Proverbs looks at a hoary head (gray hair) as a "crown of glory; it is gained in a righteous life" (Prov. 16:31, *RSV*). Old age, says the psalmist, should be productive. "They will still yield fruit in old age; they shall be full of sap and very green" (Ps. 92:14).

Grandparents are to teach godly values to their grandchildren. "Only give heed to yourself and keep your soul diligently, lest you forget the things which your eyes have seen, and lest they depart from your heart all the days of your life; but make them known to your sons and your grandsons" (Deut. 4:9).

Lois, the only woman the Bible specifically calls grandmother, taught Timothy the Scriptures. It was this early training that made Timothy so useful to the apostle Paul. "I am reminded of your sincere faith, a faith that dwelt first in your grandmother Lois and your mother Eunice and now, I am sure, dwells in you" (2 Tim. 1:5, *RSV*).

This Scripture can also be a comfort to women with unbelieving husbands. Timothy's father was a Greek— quite possibly an unbeliever. In this case Timothy was successfully taught the principles of the faith by his mother and grandmother.

**Reflect and Respond**
1. Complete the following sentence: "I believe a biblically and psychologically sound philosophy of discipline should include the following (write several words, phrases or sentences):

2. Proverbs 22:6 says "Train up a child in the way he should go, even when he is old he will not depart from

it." In what specific areas do you feel a child needs to be trained?

3. How well do you feel parents are "training" their children in your church?

4. How important do you feel it is to equip families to communicate effectively?

5. How do you feel the single adults in your church would rate the church's ministry to them in terms of meeting their needs in specific ways? Circle one:

poor    fair    good    excellent

6. How do you feel the elderly people in your church would rate the church's ministry to them in terms of meeting their needs in specific ways? Circle one:

poor    fair    good    excellent

7. Is your family a model of quality family relationships? Do your church leaders model quality family relationships for other families in your church?

### Area 4—Family Teaching

By family teaching we mean the teaching of biblical principles within the home. Very early in the Bible, parents are given the responsibility for teaching godly values to their children. In Genesis it was said of Abram,

"For I have chosen him, in order that he may command his children and his household after him to keep the way of the Lord" (Gen. 18:19).

A "how to" model for teaching biblical values to children is given in Deuteronomy 6:4-9. Moses, instructing parents how they are to teach their children in the Promised Land, lays down three basic principles.

*First, parents are to love God with all their heart and to have His laws in their hearts* (see vv. 5,6). This means modeling or teaching by example and is the foundation of all teaching. Jesus emphasized the importance of teaching by example when He said that "everyone when he is fully taught will be like his teacher" (Luke 6:40, *RSV*).

*Secondly, parents are to take these words of God that are in their own hearts and "teach them diligently" to their children* (Deut. 6:7). In the Hebrew, "teach diligently" denotes a formal type of instruction—something specific that the parent is to teach his children.

There is a third principle mentioned in this passage. Hebrew parents were to "talk" of them (God's laws) "when you sit in your house and when you walk by the way and when you lie down and when you rise up" (v. 7). This is informal teaching—teaching from all of life— whenever and wherever we can.

God's basic plan for passing His values from generation to generation is by parents teaching their own children. The psalmist says: "He established a testimony in Jacob, and appointed a law in Israel, which he commanded our fathers to teach to their children; that the next generation might know them, the children yet unborn, and arise and tell them to their children, so that they should set their hope in God, and not forget the works of God, but keep his commandments" (Ps. 78:5-7, *RSV*).

Fathers are depicted as the spiritual leaders of the home—the lead teachers—throughout the Bible. (See Ps. 78; Col. 3:21; Eph. 6:4.) Mothers are also shown to be a part of this teaching team. "Hear, my son, your father's instruction, and reject not your mother's teaching" (Prov. 1:8, *RSV*).

In the absence of a godly father, the mother is shown as the primary teacher of values. Paul writing to Timothy says, "I am reminded of your sincere faith, a faith that dwelt first in your grandmother Lois and your mother Eunice and now, I am sure, dwells in you" (2 Tim. 1:5, *RSV*).

The teaching of Christian values is a responsibility given to parents by God. Educational agencies of the church should equip parents for their God-given task and support the Christian teaching in the home.

### Reflect and Respond

1. The author states that "the teaching of Christian values to children by parents is a God-given responsibility," and that "educational agencies of the church should equip parents and support their Christian teaching at home."

a. Do you agree or disagree with this statement?


b. Estimate how many families in your church actually teach their children according to Deuteronomy 6:4-9?


c. Estimate how many families are expecting educational agencies of the church to do the teaching for them?

2. Which of the three principles of teaching given in Deuteronomy 6:4-9 do you feel is the hardest for parents to apply? Why?

3. Do you feel, that for the most part, fathers in your church are the spiritual leaders in their families? What are some reasons they are or are not spiritual leaders to their families?

4. Do you consistently teach your children according to Deuteronomy 6:4-9?

### Area 5—Family in Ministry

The church is an extension of Christ's ministry on earth. The family, the church in miniature, is also an extension of that ministry. Paul, writing to the church at Colossae, says, "And whatever you do or say, let it be as a representative of the Lord Jesus, and come with him into the presence of God the Father to give Him your thanks" (Col. 3:17, *TLB*).

As "representatives" of Christ our families have a responsibility to minister in three major areas.

*The family is to minister by witnessing to those outside of Christ.* Jesus' instructions to His disciples should be carried out by all Christians. "Go therefore and make disciples of all nations, baptizing them in the name of the Father and of the Son and of the Holy Spirit, teaching them to observe all that I have commanded you; and lo, I am with you always, to the close of the age" (Matt. 28:19,20, *RSV*).

The family, as a unit, can be a crucial force to win "all nations" to Christ as family members reach out to neighbors and to missions around the world.

*The family is to minister by setting an example for those outside of Christ.* As representatives of Christ, families have a great responsibility to be an example to those outside the church. Paul stresses the importance of the Christian's example to the non-Christian in Colossians 4:5,6. "Conduct yourself wisely toward outsiders, making the most of the time. Let your speech always be gracious, seasoned with salt, so that you may know how you ought to answer every one" *(RSV)*.

Peter reminds the Christians that they should maintain "good conduct" among the Gentiles and then gives them specific examples: "Be careful how you behave among your unsaved neighbors; . . . for the Lord's sake, obey every law of your government: . . . It is God's will that your good lives should silence those who foolishly condemn the Gospel without knowing what it can do for them, having never experienced its power" (1 Pet. 2:12-15, *TLB*).

Jesus also taught that good relationship with everyone was important. The second greatest commandment, Jesus said, was to "love your neighbor as yourself" (Matt. 22:36-40).

In Matthew 5:38-48 Jesus gave ways this love to neighbors was to be expressed. A proper response to those who are not friends was emphasized. "Don't resist those who are evil but if they strike you turn the other cheek" (see vv. 38,39). "If someone wants your coat, give them your cloak also. If they force you to go one mile, go two miles with them" (see vv. 40,41). "Love your enemies and pray for those who persecute you.

Salute, [treat friendly] all persons, not just your friends" (see v. 47).

*The family is to minister within the church.* The apostle Paul in Ephesians 4:12 says that Christians are to be equipped for ministry so they can build up the Body of Christ. Love is at the heart of an upbuilding ministry. "Love one another with brotherly affection; outdo one another in showing honor" (Rom. 12:10, *RSV*).

The family can minister in love in many specific ways. By bearing one another's burdens (see Gal. 6:2); by encouraging leaders, the weak, the fainthearted, and "always doing good to one another and to all" (1 Thess. 5:11-15).

To minister effectively, the family must develop a servant's heart—a heart that is continually looking for needs and trying to meet them. Jesus set the example for servanthood in word and action. When His disciples questioned Him about greatness He answered, "But it shall not be so among you; but whoever would be great among you must be your servant, and whoever would be first among you must be slave of all. For the Son of man also came not to be served but to serve, and give his life as a ransom for many" (Mark 10:43-45, *RSV*).

A servant family can minister by praying for others. "First of all, then," says Paul, "I urge that supplications, prayers, intercessions, and thanksgivings be made for all men" (1 Tim. 2:1, *RSV*).

Each person within the family should be encouraged to use his God-given spiritual gift in the church and in serving others. "Having gifts that differ according to the grace given to us, let us use them" (Rom. 12:6, *RSV*).

The Scriptures also urge families to, "contribute to the needs of the saints, practice hospitality" (Rom. 12: 13, *RSV*).

Families in ministry—meeting needs in the spirit of

31

Christ—can add a tremendous dimension of love to the Body of Christ.

## Reflect and Respond

1. Rate the families in your church in each area of ministry the author suggests. Circle the word you feel is most accurate.

a. Families witness to those outside of Christ.

        never    seldom    sometimes    often

b. Families set an example for those outside of Christ.

        never    seldom    sometimes    often

c. Families minister within the church.

        never    seldom    sometimes    often

2. List some ways you feel families could be encouraged to minister in these three areas.

3. Does your family set an example for other families in witness, example and ministry within the church?

# 2

# Determining Family Needs in Your Church

In 1973 a major Sunday School publishing house decided to increase its help to families. The first question the publisher considered was: "What kind of help do families need?"

To find answers to this crucial question a questionnaire was designed that zeroed in on 12 key concerns of families. Responses to the questionnaire came from 1000 men and women across the United States.[1] Here are the results.

### What Kind of Help Do Families Need?

| Interested | | Crucial |
|---|---|---|
| 788 | Communication in the family | 218 |
| 736 | Teach children Christian values | 138 |
| 688 | Discipline of children (how, how much) | 124 |
| 623 | Plans for family devotions | 98 |

The questionnaire determined that the most needy areas were: (1) communication in the family; (2) teaching children Christian values; (3) discipline of children; (4) plans for family devotions. This survey information played an important role in the development of *Family Life Today*, a magazine designed to meet the needs of the family.[2]

To help families in your church you must *first know their needs*. In what areas of family life do your families need to be equipped? What are their specific needs? How can you determine those needs? These are questions that every church leader who desires to successfully minister to families must answer.

As I see it, there are three basic ways church leaders can determine family needs.

• First is by *observation*. This means discovering needs by what you see and hear. By this I mean *active* observation—watching the way family members relate to one another; listening to those who have family problems; being sensitive to the many family needs around you.

• Second is *gathering specific information* by surveys— informally gathering information as well as interviewing people and using questionnaires.

• Third is *gathering general information* from magazine articles, newspaper stories, national polls and current books. In other words, being alert to what is happening to families nationwide so that you are seeing "the big family picture."

## Determine Family Needs by Observation

A pastor friend of mine, Martin Lee, is a good example of what I mean. Martin observed that in his church there were a number of widows with real needs. He became convinced from Scripture that the church should care about those needs and try to meet them.

Martin called each widow in his church and invited her to a luncheon. Many widows accepted the invitation. After lunch Martin shared with them how Scripture told of God's personal love and care of widows. He then asked what specific needs they had.

"I was amazed at the needs that were expressed," Martin told me. "There were leaky faucets, water in basements, roof problems, light fixtures that hadn't worked in months as well as inadequate or broken plumbing."

Martin promptly shared with his deacons the needs of all these widows and his vision to help them. The deacons caught his enthusiasm and soon these nitty-gritty needs were met. "Some of the widows just couldn't believe what was being done for them," Martin commented.

The widows' spiritual and social needs were also met. Trips were arranged for them. Each widow, who desired, had a church family assigned to her for a year. It was the sponsoring family's responsibility to send the widow a birthday card, provide transportation when needed—to be a loving, caring family.

Notice Martin's progression in determining the needs

of the widows. He observed their needs. Next he created a situation where he could ask for specific information about their needs. In other words, he observed and he gathered specific information.

## Determine Needs by Gathering Specific Information

*Surveys:* Specific information about family needs can be obtained by using a variety of survey methods. You can meet with special groups within the church and have them tell you their needs. For example, you can meet with a young married couples' class or senior citizens' class at the Sunday School hour. Or, you can invite the singles in your church to an evening dessert and have them share their needs with you. You can gain valuable information in this way. One drawback, however, is that some of the deepest family needs may not be shared in this kind of setting.

When I started as minister of family life at the Christian Church in Beaverton, Oregon, my first step in determining family needs was to meet with about 40 key people of the congregation. I asked each person to list what they felt were the five greatest needs of families in the church. We talked about those lists and several major areas of need emerged as we talked together. This was an *informal survey.*

An *interview* is another way of gathering information on family needs. The interview can be simple—limited to just two questions: (1) What do you see as the three biggest needs of families in our church? (2) What do you feel we could do to meet these needs? A good thing about this approach is that there is personal contact and interaction between the interviewer and the person being interviewed. Also, these two questions often trigger responses that reveal areas of need that the person would not normally share in a larger group.

A weakness of the *interview-survey* method is that some persons may feel reluctant to express their true feelings in face-to-face conversation.

One of the most effective ways to obtain specific information about family needs in the church is to have teenagers and adults in your congregation fill out a *questionnaire*. There is a questionnaire included in this chapter that will help you determine family needs in the five major areas of need I have defined in the introduction of this book.

The best way to administer such a questionnaire is to have people fill it out while at church—in a Sunday School class or some other meeting where a large number of the church members are present. Maybe you will want to use the questionnaire as part of a Sunday School session. It can be given at a later date to those who are absent.

Another way to use the questionnaire is to mail it to the persons you want to survey. This will work, but it takes considerable more follow-up as people are slow in mailing their responses.

Note that you can use the following questionnaire for adults and for young people from ages 12 to 18. Special instructions for young people are included on the questionnaire. Make sufficient copies of the questionnaire to survey the members of your congregation.

### Family Life Questionnaire

Dear Family Member:

We want to enrich the family life of persons in our church and community. To do this we need to identify family needs. By responding to the statements on the following questionnaire you can help us determine these needs.

We do *not* want names on these questionnaires. The results of your questionnaire will be combined with others to give us a comprehensive view of family life needs in our church.

In the questionnaire you will find 51 statements on various aspects of family life. Read each statement and indicate the level of need *you feel in your family* by circling one of the numbers to the right. If the statement does apply, circle the number that best represents the level of need in your family. For example if you feel that a statement only slightly represents a needy area in your family, circle number 1. If the statement represents a very important need in your family, circle number 4. Indicate moderate levels of need by circling numbers 2 or 3.

*Instructions for Young People (12-18):* Read the above instructions. Then respond to as many statements as possible on this questionnaire. Some will not directly apply to you. However, when a statement does not directly apply to you always ask yourself: "Do my parents have a need in this area?" or "Do we need this in our family?" For example when you respond to statements on husband-wife relationships, think: "Do my parents need this in their marriage?" and circle a number.

Give the Following Information by Circling Items That Apply:
*Age:* 12-18   19-25   26-32   33-40   41-50   51-62   63+
*Sex:* Male   Female
*Marital Status:* Single   Married   Divorced   Widowed

*Area 1—Personal Relationship with God*

| | Does not apply | | low | | high |
|---|---|---|---|---|---|
| 1. Teaching that will help me apply Scripture to my daily life | 0 | 1 | 2 | 3 | 4 |
| 2. Teaching on doctrine (salvation, grace, Holy Spirit, etc.) | 0 | 1 | 2 | 3 | 4 |
| 3. Opportunity to share and learn in small groups | 0 | 1 | 2 | 3 | 4 |

4. One person to take a personal interest in me and help me grow toward Christian maturity    0   1   2   3   4

5. Verse by verse study of books of the Bible    0   1   2   3   4

6. Increased knowledge of basics of the Christian faith    0   1   2   3   4

7. How to establish an effective devotional life    0   1   2   3   4

8. How to better handle my emotions (anger, fear, etc.)    0   1   2   3   4

9. How to establish a positive self-image    0   1   2   3   4

10. How to arrange the priorities in my life    0   1   2   3   4

*Area 2—Husband-Wife Relationships*

11. How to have better communication in marriage    0   1   2   3   4

12. How to work out appropriate husband-wife roles    0   1   2   3   4

13. Better balance on how my spouse and I make decisions    0   1   2   3   4

14. Share openly with each other    0   1   2   3   4

15. How to handle conflict in a Christian manner    0   1   2   3   4

16. How to have a regular time of husband-wife devotions    0   1   2   3   4

17. Guidelines for sexual happiness in marriage    0   1   2   3   4

18. How to set goals in marriage    0   1   2   3   4

19. How to grow in oneness    0   1   2   3   4

20. Biblical teaching on marriage    0   1   2   3   4

21. Family finances/how to handle money    0   1   2   3   4

22. Small group interaction with other couples on marriage    0 1 2 3 4

*Area 3—Family Relationships*

23. How to effectively discipline my children    0 1 2 3 4
24. How to build a positive self-image in my children    0 1 2 3 4
25. Things to do, places to go as a family    0 1 2 3 4
26. How to schedule more time for the family    0 1 2 3 4
27. How to build a better relationship with my children    0 1 2 3 4
28. Better communication within the family    0 1 2 3 4
29. How to handle family conflict in a Christian manner    0 1 2 3 4
30. Programs, teaching and other opportunities that focus on the single adult    0 1 2 3 4
31. A ministry to widows    0 1 2 3 4
32. How to prepare for retirement/ help for the middle years    0 1 2 3 4
33. How to be a better grandparent    0 1 2 3 4
34. Ministry to those over 60    0 1 2 3 4
35. Biblical teaching on family relationships    0 1 2 3 4
36. How to build good relationships with in-laws    0 1 2 3 4
37. Help for the one-parent family    0 1 2 3 4

*Area 4—Family Teaching*

38. How to teach Christian values to my children by my example    0 1 2 3 4

39. How to teach Christian values to 0   1   2   3   4
    my children in an informal way
40. How to teach Christian values to 0   1   2   3   4
    my children by family nights,
    devotions and other types of
    structured teaching times
41. How to teach my children the   0   1   2   3   4
    basics of the Christian faith
42. How to lead my children to Christ 0   1   2   3   4
43. How to help my children establish 0   1   2   3   4
    a devotional life
44. How to help my children establish 0   1   2   3   4
    Christian friendships and choose
    a Christian marriage partner
45. How to prepare my children for   0   1   2   3   4
    adolescence
46. How to enable my children to be 0   1   2   3   4
    a success
47. How to talk about sex with my   0   1   2   3   4
    children

*Area 5—Family in Ministry*
48. Projects, ideas and motivation   0   1   2   3   4
    to help our family serve within
    the church
49. Projects, ideas and motivation to 0   1   2   3   4
    help our family serve within the
    neighborhood and community
50. Helps on how our family can be 0   1   2   3   4
    an example to others
51. How to witness as a family     0   1   2   3   4

To evaluate the questionnaire responses follow this step-by-step procedure:

1. Separate the adult and youth responses. Compute each group separately.

2. Compute the total responses for each of the 51 statements—add together all numbers circled for each statement on all of the questionnaires.

3. Write the total of all responses to the left of each statement. Continue this procedure until you have the total number of responses for each statement. For example:

---

*Area 1—Personal Relationship with God*

Totals

|  | | Does not apply | low | | high |
|---|---|---|---|---|---|
| (119) | 1. Teaching that will help me apply Scripture to my daily life | 0  1 | 2  3 | 4 |
| (72) | 2. Teaching on doctrine (salvation grace, Holy Spirit, etc.) | 0  1 | 2  3 | 4 |

---

4. Note that those statements with the largest totals will be the areas of greatest felt need in your church.

5. Consider carefully the special groups in your congregation. *Totals only* do not accurately reflect the needs of some groups. For example, the total of all responses for "a ministry to widows" (statement 31 on the questionnaire), might be only 42. However, if there are just 12 widows in your congregation this would indicate a significant need.

6. Thoughtfully evaluate the totals. List totals for each statement with the largest number at the top of the list. Determine the five most needy areas in your church by noting the five statements with the largest totals. Place an asterisk by statements where score does not clearly indicate level of need, such as widows, singles, grandparents, etc.

7. Compare the needs indicated by the adult responses and those indicated by the responses of the teenagers. In what way are they alike? How do they differ?

## Determine Needs by Gathering General Information

The third basic way of discovering family needs in your church is by gathering general information about the family. What are nationwide polls saying about the family? Are magazines indicating family trends and needs? What is your local newspaper reporting about the family? What are current books saying about the family today? General information from such sources can help us get the "big picture" of what is happening to families nationwide. This in turn makes us more conscious of family needs in our local churches.

For example, *U.S. News and World Report*, in a recent issue, focused on trends in families in the United States. Here are some of the highlights:

*In 1960, there were 26 divorces for every 100 marriages. Today, there are 48 divorces for every 100 marriages. By 1990, based on trends, there will be 63 divorces for every 100 marriages.*[3]

What needs do these facts indicate? What does this say about the need for premarital teaching and counseling within the church? What does this say about the need for ongoing marriage enrichment provided by the church?

*More than 30% of school age children are living with parents who have been divorced at least once . . . . One sixth of all U.S. children under 18 live in one-parent families.*[4]

What needs are indicated here? How does the church need to help those who divorce and remarry to adjust to

43

the pressures of this new life? What type of training and encouragement do divorced parents need? What help will the children need? What are the needs of the one-parent family? What support and training does the single parent need? What can the church do for the children of one-parent families?

In "The Report on the American Family," a survey of attitudes and opinions of 340,374 persons conducted by *Better Homes and Gardens*, the following interesting opinions were expressed. Seventy-nine percent of the respondents felt that the dominant role of the husband in the American family is declining in importance. Seventy-one percent of the respondents felt that this decline was bad. The respondents were also asked, "In your family, who has the major responsibility for disciplining the youngsters?" Fifty-eight percent said the mother had the major responsibility.

Another interesting question was, "Do you feel the father in most families spends enough time with the youngsters?" An overwhelming 87 percent of the respondents said no.[5]

What does this report indicate about needs that might have to be met in your church? Do fathers know what their biblical role should be? Do fathers in your church need training on how to be spiritual leaders at home? Why do you feel that most of the respondents felt fathers do not spend enough time with the youngsters? How could this affect the spiritual training of the children? Family solidarity? Communication? Does the church need to have an ongoing program to train fathers in any of these areas?

*The Report to the President: White House Conference on Children* points to many family needs in the United States, one of which is for children to have cross-generational interaction.

*And here we confront a fundamental and disturbing fact:* Children need people in order to become human. *The fact is fundamental because it is firmly grounded both in scientific research and in human experience. It is disturbing because the isolation of children from adults simultaneously threatens the growth of the individual and the survival of the society. The young cannot pull themselves up by their own bootstraps. It is primarily through observing, playing and working with others older and younger than himself that a child discovers both what he can do and who he can become—that he develops both his ability and his identity. It is primarily through exposure and interaction with adults and children of different ages that a child requires new interests and skills and learns the meaning of tolerance, cooperation, and compassion. Hence to relegate children to a world of their own is to deprive them of their humanity, and ourselves as well.*[6]

Does this report indicate any needs in our churches? Do we isolate children from adults? Young adults from senior citizens? Is our closely graded method of education always best for families? Is there some way that we can bring generations together in education and worship?

Twenty-eight years ago Oregon High school seniors were surveyed about their opinions and experiences. That survey was revised and given to Oregon high school seniors last year. One particular item stood out. In 1948, 82 percent of the respondents said their families engaged in leisure activities as a group. Last year, only 24.5 percent of the youths said they did things together as a family "often." Another 48 percent said they participated in family activities "sometimes" while 19 percent said they seldom had such activities and another 3.5 percent said such activities "never" happened.[7]

Does this survey indicate a need for families to examine their priorities and schedules? Is it important for families to do things together? Does your church help or hinder family unity? Do families need to be trained and motivated to do things together?

A recent study by two Johns Hopkins University researchers shows a dramatic 30 percent increase in the sexual activity among unmarried girls in the last five years. Professors Melvin Zelnik and John Kantner report that over half of all 19-year-old single women are "sexually experienced."[8]

Does this say something about moral training within families? What can the church do to help parents communicate Christian life-styles to their children? Do parents need to be equipped to talk about sex with their children? What type of support system does the church need to provide for young people who are confronted daily with liberal sexual views?

This is the kind of general information on the family that may point to family needs in your church. There is much more information available. Be on the alert constantly for information on the family. Always ask the question, "What does this information indicate about family needs in our church?"

In this chapter we have discussed three ways of determining family needs in your church: (1) by observation; (2) by gathering specific information by surveys; and (3) by being alert and looking for general information about families in current publications. The church leader who uses a combination of these three methods will gain a comprehensive view of family needs in his church.

**Reflect and Respond**

1. List five family needs that you have observed in your congregation.

2. Rank the five needs in order of priority.

3. List ways leaders in your church have opportunities to informally gather specific information about family needs.

4. If you could concentrate on just two family needs in your church during the next 12 months, what would they be?

## 5. List three specific needs you feel in your own family.

---

**Notes**

1. Survey conducted by *Family Life Today*, Gospel Light Publications, Glendale, California. Questionnaire respondents were participants in seminars conducted by International Center for Learning, the teacher training arm of Gospel Light Publications.
2. *Family Life Today*, a monthly magazine published by Gospel Light Publications, 110 W. Broadway, Glendale, California 91204.
3. "The American Family: Can It Survive Today's Shocks?" *U.S. News & World Report* (October 27, 1975), p. 32.
4. "The American Family," p. 41.
5. "The Report on the American Family," *Better Homes and Gardens* (October, 1972).
6. *Report to the President: White House Conference on Children* (U.S. Government Printing Office, Washington, D.C., 1971), p. 242.
7. Rod Patterson, "Governor's Commission on Youth: 1976 High School Opinion and Attitude Survey," *The Oregonian* (January 2, 1977), pp. A-1, D-6.
8. Donald Zochert, Chicago Daily News Service, *The Oregonian* (April 11, 1977), p. C-3.

# 3
# How to Organize and Plan Your Family Ministry

All ministries within a church require organization and planning. Organization is merely grouping tasks in an orderly fashion to get a job done. Planning enables us to take the necessary steps to achieve our purposes and goals.

The purpose of this chapter is to help you organize and plan for a church ministry that meets the needs of families. There are no "average" churches nor "typical" organizational structures, so adapt the ideas in this chapter to fit your own situation.

Here are eight steps that I feel are essential in organizing and planning your family ministry:

### Step 1—Share Your Vision with Church Leadership

Whoever you are in the church—whether a church staff member directly responsible for family ministry, or a layman wanting to help your church minister more effectively to families, it is essential that church leadership catch your vision. There are several reasons for this. Churches usually focus on what the leadership feels is important. If the people holding leadership positions in your church (staff, elders, deacons, board and committee chairmen, etc.) feel that it is a high priority to minister to specific family needs, the chances for a vital family ministry are great. If, however, only a few people take on the task by themselves with little involvement from leadership, the chances of an effective ministry to families are slim.

A second reason why a shared vision with leadership is important is that people like to feel a part of what is going on. Your family ministry will need a broad base of involvement and support to be successful.

There is a third and vital reason why it is necessary to share your family ministry vision with church leadership. *Both church programming and church leaders* must model biblically sound family principles. A church that says it wants to meet the needs of families and yet fragments families by its busy, age-segregated scheduling is contradicting itself. It is saying that families *are not* all that important. People will believe what they see happening. Actions do speak louder than words!

If a church emphasizes and teaches biblical family principles and leaders do not have healthy family relationships, again there is a glaring contradiction. The effectiveness of what is taught will be impaired by what people see in the lives of the leaders.

As leaders we are to teach by the example of our lives. *This includes family life.* The power of teaching by example is awesome. Think of your children for a moment. Have you ever tried to teach your children a principle that you were not practicing in your own life? Which did they follow—your instruction or your example? Jesus Himself said, "Everyone, after he has been fully trained, will be like his teacher" (Luke 6:40). And Paul said, "Follow my example as I follow Christ's" (1 Cor. 11:1, *NEB*).

The ideal would be every church leader living out with his family the principles of family living that are taught in the Bible and each leader setting a good example for other families in the church. We are not talking about *perfect* examples. There are no perfect people or *perfect* families. We are talking about families who have problems but find solutions to their problems in God's Word; families who have good family relationships because of their commitment to one another, to biblical principles and to God.

Make an appointment to share your family ministry vision with your board of elders, board of deacons, Christian education committee or whatever agencies of your church you feel are most appropriate. Make your presentation very positive. It would be best to focus on the need and your church's potential for meeting family needs.

Do not lay out a comprehensive plan for a family ministry at this initial meeting. That will come later. Coming on too strong too soon may turn some people off. Some people may not share your enthusiasm for ministering to families. It is very possible that you will get some strong negative reactions to your vision of a concentrated ministry to families. Some people will simply not see the need. In many cases I have found this blind spot in individuals who were not successful with their own families.

Others may see a ministry to families as a threat to "regular" church programs. These people see a family emphasis as competing with the more traditional ministries such as evangelism, vacation Bible school, youth programs, etc. It is important to help your church leadership see that such competition does not exist. Strong families make strong churches. A major purpose of a family ministry is to equip families to minister effectively in the church and the community.

There are additional purposes for this initial meeting. You need to arouse interest and concern for families. And you need to get official sanction to enlist a group of people to study the family needs of your congregation and to make a report to the appropriate group or board.

## Step 2—Organize a Family Life Committee

The size and personality of your family life committee will reflect the size of your church. Here are some general guidelines, however, that you may adapt to your situation.

There are several qualifications I suggest you look for in the people you recruit to serve on your family life committee. First, they should have a growing personal relationship with God. Second, they should be deeply committed to their own families. The results of this commitment should be visible. It should be obvious that the family is practicing godly principles of family living with the product of loving, caring family relationships. The people you recruit should also have a desire to help other families.

Another requirement is that these people should not be already loaded down with other responsibilities within the church. This makes recruiting difficult because of the 20-80 principle that is found in most churches—20 percent of the people doing 80 percent of the work!

In my church experiences I have observed people with successful families who would have made good committee members but I chose not to recruit them because they were already overly involved. I felt it would be contradictory to recruit them to a family ministry that would keep them away from their own families.

For example, in one church where I worked the person I wanted for the family life committee chairman taught a class, was Christian education committee chairman and was a member of the church board. As we talked about his ministry in the church, Rich said that his real interest and commitment was to help families. The problem was that he already was busy with these other responsibilities. We decided together if he was to become chairman of the family life committee he should step down as Christian education committee chairman.

I feel that all persons recruited for the family life committee should be asked not to take on additional responsibilities during the year. Committee work will keep them busy enough. We want them to model successful family principles. They can do this only if they spend adequate time with their families.

A good balance is essential for a family life committee. You should recruit people that represent a variety of interests and family life-styles. A family life committee of young adults, for example, would be primarily interested in family matters regarding young families— discipline, family times, marriage adjustment, etc. It would be possible for them to overlook needs of the elderly, widows, divorced and middle-aged.

An ideal committee might include the following: a young couple, both about 23; a couple age 32 with children 3,5 and 9; a middle-aged couple and a couple over 65; a widow, a divorced person and a person who has never been married.

On such a committee a wide variety of needs and interests will be represented. This should enable you to plan and organize a well-balanced family ministry. You could have certain people on the committee be responsible for specific areas of the ministry. For example, a family life committee in one church has one couple in charge of family teaching (helping people get started having family nights, etc.) and another couple who is in charge of marriage enrichment.

Consider having your committee members bring their entire families to the meetings. Older children can take care of the younger children or you can hire a babysitter for times when the adults need to be alone. Our children look back on some of our family life committee meetings with fond memories. They remember happy meetings that were really family affairs.

### Step 3—State Your Own Biblical Basis for a Family Ministry

After you have formed your family life committee, take time to think through together the biblical basis for the work you are doing. Begin by having each committee member read the introduction and chapter 1 of this book, *How to Help the Christian Home*.

Make available to committee members the following books that deal with biblical teachings concerning the family: *The Measure of a Family*, Gene Getz; *Facing the Future—the Church and Family Together*, edited by Gary Collins; *Heaven Help the Home!*, Howard Hendricks; and *Family Living in the Bible*, Edith Deen.

Have a meeting when you can discuss this material. Pray for guidance and together work out a written statement of what the committee feels is the biblical basis for the family ministry of your church.

### Step 4—Determine Family Needs

The family life committee should make a comprehensive study of the family needs in your church. All committee members need to study chapter 2 of this book and become familiar with the three methods of determining family needs: *observation; surveys that gather specific family information;* and the *gathering of general family information.*

Decide on the approach or approaches your committee will take to determine the family needs in your church. Discuss how and when you can effectively use the "Family Life Questionnaire" (see chap. 2).

When you have gathered adequate information on family needs in your church have your committee review the findings. Make a list of the most important family needs by arranging the needs in order, with the highest priority needs at the top of the list.

Now you are ready to identify key purposes for family ministry in your congregation.

## Step 5—Establishing Purposes

Do you remember the diagram in the introduction of this book? Let's look at it again.

According to this formula for an effective family ministry in the church, *purposes are based on the needs of the congregation.*

Let's say that your congregation has responded to the "Family Life Questionnaire" (see chap. 2). And that your family life committee has evaluated the computed responses. You have discovered that the responses to "Area 2—Husband-Wife Relationships" reveal a real need. In fact, the statement "How to have better communication in marriage" has scored the highest of all statements on the questionnaire.

This is the evidence you need for deciding to establish the purpose: *To enable couples to have better communication in marriage.* Remember, when you establish a purpose you are stating a direction your family ministry will take. You are stating an aim that will help you set specific goals.

**Worksheets for Family Ministry**

At the end of this chapter you will find a section of worksheets that can be reproduced for use in your committee.

"Worksheet 1—Establishing Purposes Worksheet" will guide you as you list your specific purposes under each *Area of Family Need.* When you have completed the listing you will have a comprehensive view of the direction that your family ministry will take in the coming months.

After you have established your purpose, have your committee prepare a report that includes: the committee's biblical basis for family ministry; your assessment of family needs in the church; and the purposes you have established. Present your report to an appropriate leadership body in your church. It would be helpful if the report could be duplicated and handed out to those attending this meeting.

Have a thorough discussion of the report. Suggest that the leadership body officially accept the biblical basis and purposes of a family ministry and commission the family life committee to plan and organize to meet those needs and purposes.

## Step 6—Set Goals and Priorities

By now you should know what you want to accomplish in your family ministry: *your purposes.* The next step is to set goals that will make it possible for you to accomplish those purposes. The goals should be specific activities or happenings that are both measurable and accomplishable.

Earlier in this chapter, when we talked about establishing purposes, we used the example that one purpose might be: *To enable couples to have better communication in marriage.* Goals to accomplish this purpose could be:

• Goal 1—Conduct a couples' class using *Communication: Key to Your Marriage,* a study course authored by H. Norman Wright.

• Goal 2—Hold a marriage enrichment retreat in February.

• Goal 3—Schedule sermons during the year to focus on communication in marriage.

Note that the setting of goals involves planning for *definite activities.* In the worksheet section at the end of this chapter, "Worksheet 2—Goal-Priority Worksheet" will help your committee to set goals that will help you accomplish your purposes. List the goals under each purpose in order of priority.

Worksheet 3 is a "Long Range Goals Worksheet" to help you list the goals you have selected for this year and for the years to come. This sheet will help you do some advance planning and dreaming. Think and talk about: What will we want to accomplish next year? In year three of our family life program? In year four? Year five? In ten years? Of course, many of these long range goals will change, but it will strengthen your overall family ministry to occasionally project your thinking into the future.

### Step 7—Plan to Accomplish Your Goals

Planning is vital to your family ministry. Many good ideas remain just that—"good ideas"—because people fail to plan how they will achieve their goals. The success of your family ministry will depend, to a large extent, on how diligently your committee plans and then—carries out the plans.

Use the Worksheet 4—"Planning Worksheet" at the end of this chapter to help you achieve your goals. List each goal and then answer the following questions: (1) How will we accomplish this goal? (plan in detail!); (2) who will be responsible? (assign responsibilities); (3) when will this be accomplished? (be specific).

### Step 8—Evaluate Your Goals

*Has the accomplishment of this goal moved us closer to our purpose?* This is the question the family life committee must ask about each goal as it is accomplished. You see that the goal has not helped you achieve your purpose, then you need to ask why? Do you need to change your approach? Were your resources adequate? Did you carry through on your plan? What do you need to do to better meet your purposes?

These questions can be answered only if you evaluate the goals you have achieved. In the worksheet section at the end of this chapter there are two evaluation forms that can help you evaluate your completed goals. Use "Evaluation Form 1" at the completion of each family life activity.

"Evaluation Form 2" should be given to your entire

church at the end of the year. This evaluation feedback will help you see whom you have ministered to and to what extent you have met family needs. (Note: You will need to adapt the evaluation sheet to your activities and purposes. First list *your* specific purposes and then the goals or activities you offered to strengthen families in that area.)

Let's again use the example we gave of purposes and goals concerning communication in marriage to illustrate how this evaluation works (See pp. 56–57).

| Evaluate | | Degree of Helpfulness | | | |
|---|---|---|---|---|---|
| | | low | moderate | | high |
| Purpose: *To enable couples to have better communications* | | | | | |
| Goals/Activities | | | | | |
| 1. *Conduct a couples class...* | 1 | 2 | 3 | 4 | 5 |
| 2. *Hold a marriage retreat...* | 1 | 2 | 3 | 4 | 5 |
| 3. *Sermon on marriage...* | 1 | 2 | 3 | 4 | 5 |

## Conclusion

These eight steps can help your church minister to families effectively. Remember it is important to *involve leadership* in planning your family ministry. Planning should reflect *needs*, a well thought-out *biblical basis* as well as clearly stated purposes and goals.

One word of warning here. *Don't try to do too much your first year*. It is much better to increase your ministry to families at a slow steady pace. Select several well thought-out goals for your first year. Do a good job on these. Then, evaluate and plan your strategy for the next year.

## Reflect and Respond

1. Do you agree or disagree with the author that it is

important to share your family vision with leadership in the church? Give a reason for your answer.

2. What do you feel will be the major obstacle you will have to overcome to have a successful family ministry? List at least one way this obstacle might be overcome.

3. How important do you feel it is for leaders within your church to "model" successful family principles? Why?

4. How important do you feel it is for a church's programming to model that the family is important? Why? To what extent do the programs of your church model that the family is important?

5. List some people in your church who you feel would qualify to serve on a family life committee.

## Worksheet 1—Establishing Purposes Worksheet

*Area 1—To Help Persons Build a Personal Relationship with God.*

Specific purposes
1. *to help members arrange priorites in life*
2.
3.

*Area 2—To Strengthen Husband-Wife Relationships*
Specific purposes
1. *to enable couples to have better communication in marriage*
2.
3.

*Area 3—To Encourage Healthy Family Relationships*
Specific Purposes
1. *to enable couples to build a better relationship with their children*
2.
3.

*Area 4—To Enable Parents to Teach Christian Values to Their Children*
Specific Purposes
1. *To Enable Couples to Teach Christian values to their children by example*
2.
3.

*Area 5—To Equip Families to Minister to Others*
Specific Purposes
1. *To enable the family to be an example to others*
2.
3.

## Worksheet 2—Goal-Priority Worksheet

*Area of Family Need*
  Specific Purpose   _____
    Goals to meet that purpose
      Goal 1

      Goal 2

      Goal 3


*Area of Family Need*
  Specific Purpose   _____
    Goals to meet that purpose
      Goal 1

      Goal 2

      Goal 3


*Area of Family Need*
  Specific Purpose   _____
    Goals to meet that purpose
      Goal 1

      Goal 2

      Goal 3

# Worksheet 3—Long Range Goals Worksheet

List goals in order of priority
*This Year*

*Second Year*

*Third Year*

*Fourth Year*

*Fifth Year*

*Ten Years*

## Worksheet 4—Planning Worksheet

Goal 1 _____
How will we accomplish this goal?




Who will be responsible? _____

When will we accomplish this goal? _____


Goal 2 _____
How will we accomplish this goal?




Who will be responsible? _____

When will we accomplish this goal? _____


Goal 3 _____
How will we accomplish this goal?




Who will be responsible? _____

When will we accomplish this goal? _____

## Evaluation Form 1

Age____
Marital Status: Married____ Divorced____ Single____

The purpose of this activity was to _____
_____
   (fill in specific purpose before distributing)

To what degree did this activity help to accomplish the above purpose in your family life? (circle one)

          Not at all   very little   some   very much

What portion of this activity was most helpful?


What was least helpful?


What do you feel could have been done to better meet your needs?


Other comments:

## Evaluation Form 2

Age____
Marital Status: Married____ Single____ Divorced____
   During the year we have done the following things to help families grow stronger. (Circle the number which most closely indicates the level of need the activity has met in your family life. Mark only the activities in which you were involved.)

| Evaluate | Degree of Helpfulness | | |
|---|---|---|---|
| | low | moderate | high |

Purpose: _____
Goals/Activities

| | | | | | |
|---|---|---|---|---|---|
| 1. | 1 | 2 | 3 | 4 | 5 |
| 2. | 1 | 2 | 3 | 4 | 5 |
| 3. | 1 | 2 | 3 | 4 | 5 |

Purpose: _____
Goals/Activities

| | | | | | |
|---|---|---|---|---|---|
| 1. | 1 | 2 | 3 | 4 | 5 |
| 2. | 1 | 2 | 3 | 4 | 5 |
| 3. | 1 | 2 | 3 | 4 | 5 |

Purpose: _____
Goals/Activities

| | | | | | |
|---|---|---|---|---|---|
| 1. | 1 | 2 | 3 | 4 | 5 |
| 2. | 1 | 2 | 3 | 4 | 5 |
| 3. | 1 | 2 | 3 | 4 | 5 |

The greatest need in my family life is _____
Next year I would like to see more _____

# 4
# Building a
# Personal
# Relationship
# with God

While serving as minister of family life at the Christian Church in Beaverton, Oregon, the youth minister and myself decided to conduct a parent-teen communication seminar. Why? Because we had received plenty of feedback from parents and teenagers that communication at home could be a lot better.

It seemed to us that a parent-teen communication seminar could meet some of the needs we had observed. We felt we could help parents and teens discover some positive methods of communication. But as I started to plan this seminar something seemed wrong. Then a disturbing thought hit me.

"We are starting at the wrong place, Ernie," I said to the youth minister. "I feel that there are other steps we should take before our parent-teen seminar."

"What kind of steps?" he asked with a look of surprise.

"It's been obvious to us that some of these parents do

not have a growing personal relationship with God," I pointed out. "That's where we need to start. Another thing that bothers me is that some of these couples need to strengthen their marriages. If we concentrate on those areas first, our parent-teen seminar will have a much greater chance of changing lives."

We agreed that this was the way to go and so our purposes and goals changed. We started a parents' Bible study group. Later, a number of parents enrolled in our "Growing Marriage Class." Since then we've even talked about having these two experiences as a prerequisite for parents' participation in a parent-teen seminar.

Now I am not saying that in a family ministry we should start each person at Area 1—"A Personal Relationship with God" and then go on to Area 2, and so on. Sometimes this is not practical, sometimes it is impossible. Your family ministry, however, will be more effective if you understand how one area of need relates to the other.

For example, recently I was involved in directing a marriage enrichment retreat. We did not screen people first to determine if they had a growing personal relationship with God. Some who attended were growing Christians and some were not. It was evident that most of those who were not growing Christians did not receive as much benefit from the weekend as we would have liked.

On the other hand, there was one person who had not experienced a personal relationship with God who did receive great benefit from the retreat. In fact, the weekend launched him into a whole new relationship with God and his wife. This marriage had been in trouble. The husband, an air force major and R.O.T.C. instructor, was bitter about his wife's involvement in the church.

The wife shared with me one morning. "I was really surprised when Skip said he would go to the marriage enrichment retreat with me," she continued. "But the retreat really turned him around—hearing God's principles for a happy marriage, being around committed Christian people—on the way home from the retreat he said, 'This really is the only way to go, isn't it?' "

In this case "Strengthening Husband-Wife Relationships" was the opener. The retreat brought Skip to a "Personal Relationship with God."

After the retreat, we had opportunities to help Skip as he desired to build a growing personal relationship with God. For example, we started him in the first book of the Navigators' "Design for Discipleship" series entitled *Your Life in Christ*.

In the four months since the retreat we have seen God work a miracle in that home. The wife shared with me the other day that "Every prayer request I had for my husband and family has been answered—and those requests filled a whole page."

Skip is training R.O.T.C. cadets at Fort Lewis this year with a new approach. The first words he said to his new company of cadets were, "Fellows, I am a new Christian. I am studying the Bible and trying to live Christian principles. I will probably make mistakes but I want you to know that this is where I am coming from."

## A Relationship with God and Family

Whether or not a person has a growing personal relationship with God will determine, to a large extent, whether he has a growing personal relationship with others within the family.

Howard Hendricks in his excellent book on family relationships, *Heaven Help the Home!*, gives a good example of how this spiritual principle can work:

*The closer each partner moves toward God, the closer he is to the other. Closeness brings into focus the other person, and knowing who God is helps us find out who we are. Perhaps this explains why God often has to back us into a crisis corner where we can see only Him before we get ourselves into perspective.* [1]

In the following diagram we illustrate how, when a person moves closer to God, he also moves closer to his mate.

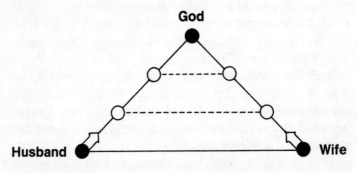

A growing personal relationship with God, then, is the foundation for all other relationships. All Christians have a personal relationship with God. Not all Christians grow at the same rate, however. But all Christians should be growing toward maturity in Christ. (Read Heb. 5:12-14; Eph. 4:13.)

What can your church do to enable persons to have a growing relationship with God? Here are a few ways to consider.

*Small Groups:* New and older Christians alike need the love, acceptance, warmth and Bible life-application that can come out of a small group Bible study. Many persons have found these groups have helped them establish a growing relationship with God. Al Wollen, pastor of the Cedar Mill Bible Church and author of *Miracles Happen in Group Bible Study*, says:

> *The church today is learning to implement and take advantage of the personal closeness in small groups in people's homes, just as the early New Testament churches did. One of the most nurturing and caring environments for healthy Christian growth is in small Bible study groups. We, as believers, must be willing to die to ourselves if we are to grow. When we honestly expose ourselves to what the Bible is saying and lovingly help each other in that exposure, then death to the self-life takes place. In order for this to happen, we have to look honestly at God's Word and see what applies to us.*[2]

Small group home Bible study is a tool any church can use to encourage growing relationships with God. I have successfully used Wollen's basic format as outlined in his book for numerous small Bible study groups. The plan is simple. Homes to host these small group studies are found in strategic locations where the church ministers. Leaders are trained. Groups are formed with a minimum of seven and a maximum of 12 persons meeting in each home.

There are two simple ground rules in each group. First, the Bible is shared in dialogue. Second, the only authority in the group is the Bible. The group covers half a chapter to a complete chapter each week. Two key questions dominate the entire study time: "What does the Bible say?" and "What does it say to me?"

Small group Bible studies such as this provide an atmosphere where an individual's personal relationship with God can grow.

*Personal Devotional Life:* Every growing Christian I

71

know has a meaningful devotional life. Communication with God through His Word and prayer are steps that move a person toward maturity in Christ. Many people have a difficult time starting and continuing a daily quiet time with God. A worthwhile purpose for any family ministry is providing individuals with materials that encourage daily devotions. The Navigators have some excellent helps in this area. One of their Bible Study series called "The 2:7 Series" can be used individually or in small groups. This course helps put Christians on a growth pattern by encouraging them to establish a quiet time as they memorize basic truths from God's Word. This series gives step-by-step information on what Scriptures to read, how to mark and apply biblical insights, how to pray effectively, and how to prepare a personal testimony. I've found that many Christians receive a great deal of help from this course.

Navigators also has a "Design for Discipleship" series of workbooks that can be used for individual or group study. These not only help a person establish a solid biblical foundation but also help set a pattern of daily Bible study and prayer.

I believe that the church's family life committee must constantly seek ways to nurture the growth of new Christians. Courses such as "The 2:7 Series," "Design for Discipleship," and *Now That I'm a Christian*, Volumes 1,2 by Chuck Miller can be useful tools.[3] Each of these resources can be used in a small group format or in a one-to-one discipleship program.

*Bible Teaching Program:* In addition to small group Bible studies, a personal Bible study and quiet time, people need good, solid verse-by-verse study of the books of the Bible. Many churches find the Sunday School hour a good time to have this type of study.

There is much good Bible-based curriculum available

from your church supplier. Choose a curriculum that stresses life application of Bible teachings. A growing personal relationship with God occurs when a person sees that God's Word is powerful and practical for his life—something he can "live-out" in everyday life.

The "Living Word" curriculum, published by Gospel Light, stresses learning by doing and the application of Scripture to a person's daily life. A curriculum such as this is vital to a strong Bible teaching program.

*Expository Preaching:* Much emphasis has been put on expository preaching in recent years. This is a clear verse-by-verse explaining of God's Word. The pastor plays an essential role in helping persons to have a growing personal relationship with God as they gain a better understanding of His Word.

*Other Growth Opportunities:* We have only mentioned a few of the many types of learning experiences that can help persons grow toward maturity in Christ. Additional opportunities include: family vacation Bible schools, summer camps, institutes in Christian living, church training programs, individual study programs, special speakers, library and media resources, all this and more can be made available to people by churches who want their people to grow in "the grace and knowledge of Jesus Christ."

*What Are the Needs of Your Church?* You will be helped to answer this question by reviewing chapter 2 "Determining Family Needs in Your Church." The first 10 statements of the "Family Life Questionnaire" in that chapter deal with the first area of family need—a personal relationship with God. These 10 statements will help you be aware of spiritual needs of people in your congregation.

Your next steps will be to define purposes and to set goals. Then you will plan ways to achieve your goals.

**You Can Start Now**

Now is the time to take some steps toward helping your people grow in their personal relationship to God. Here are idea starters:

• *Small Group Bible Studies.* All you need to get started is a commitment to the concept and a good resource like *Miracles Happen in Group Bible Study* by Albert J. Wollen.

• *Personal Prayer and Bible Study.* Decide on a specific plan to encourage people to develop a regular and vital quiet time with God. For example, begin listing devotional resources in the church bulletin.

• *Personal Growth Week.* Set aside one week during the year for a concentrated effort to inspire families to want a growing relationship with God. Provide new resources. Conduct special share and prayer groups. Include all Sunday School classes in a special Sunday of praise and thanksgiving.

• *Messages on a Relationship with God.* As a part of your "Personal Growth Week" and at other times during the year use sermons especially directed toward helping people deepen their relationship with God.

• *Note: For additional information on the resources mentioned in this chapter see "Resources for Building a Personal Relationship with God" following "Reflect and Respond."*

**Reflect and Respond**

1. Describe in a few sentences how you see the five major purposes of a family ministry relating to one another. How will this affect your family ministry?

2. Pastor Wollen says: "One of the most nurturing and caring environments for healthy Christian growth is in

small groups." Do you agree or disagree with his statement? How do you see small groups fitting into your family ministry?

3. How much do you know about the personal devotional life of the people in your church? Do they need help in establishing quiet times? Do they know how and what to read in the Bible? Do they know how to pray? Do they know how to respond to Scripture and apply it to their lives? What can the church do to help?

4. What evidence do you see in your Bible teaching program that teaching is producing change in lives?

5. List two or three things you feel are evidence that a Christian has a growing personal relationship with God.

6. Do the leaders in your church show in their lives that they are growing Christians? Explain your answer.

---

**Notes**

1. Howard Hendricks, *Heaven Help the Home!* (Wheaton: Victor Books, 1973), pp. 30,31.
2. Albert J. Wollen, *Miracles Happen in Group Bible Study* (Glendale, CA: Regal Books, 1976), p. 24.
3. Chuck Miller, *Now That I'm a Christian*, volumes 1 and 2 (Glendale, CA: Regal Books, 1976).

# 5
# Strengthening Husband-Wife Relationships

The greatest responsibility and challenge of a family ministry is to strengthen husband-wife relationships because the key to a happy family life is a strong, thriving marriage. Today there are many excellent tools available to help the church enrich good marriages and provide resources to strengthen weak marriages.

Every church should work toward offering three types of help to strengthen husband-wife relationships: (1) premarital counseling or classes; (2) marriage counseling should be available for those with troubled marriages; (3) marriage enrichment education for everyone.

How much emphasis you place on each of these areas will be determined by the needs of your church. What needs have you observed? Take a close look at the responses to the "Husband-Wife Relationships" section of the Family Life Questionnaire. What areas of need do you see?

Keep the needs of your church in mind as we look at each of the three following areas.

### Premarital Counseling

I cannot emphasize the importance of this area enough. We simply must give all our young people extensive premarital counseling if we wish to reverse the trend of weak and broken marriages. Recently a young couple to whom I had just given their fifth hour of premarital counseling decided to postpone their marriage plans and date others. These were mature Christian young people who had known each other for several years. But after talking things over in our counseling sessions they decided, on their own, that they simply were not sure that they should get married.

According to H. Norman Wright, in his book *Premarital Counseling*, this assisting couples to make their final decision is one of the purposes of premarital counseling. As he says, "We need to assist the couple in making their final decision: should we marry?"[1]

Important learning occurs in premarital counseling as couples receive critical marriage relationship information, discover their own strengths and weaknesses, correct faulty information and see God's best for marriage.

In his book, Wright suggests a minimum of six hours of premarital counseling for each couple. My first reaction was, "Sure, but what do I do with these kids for six hours?" The book answered this question by providing a thorough step-by-step plan for each premarital counseling session. It is simple. The steps work. The book also suggests testing materials and how to use them. I heartily recommend this simple but complete premarital counseling program that any church leader can use. Plans for both private and group premarital sessions are provided in the book.

## Marriage Counseling

A church that wants to minister to families must offer counseling for those with troubled marriages. Following are resources that I have found helpful in this area.

H. Norman Wright has developed a cassette training series called *Upon This Foundation* (Christian Marriage Enrichment, Denver). Volume 2 is entitled "Marriage and Family Counseling." These cassettes and accompanying workbook provide excellent training in the basics of marriage and family counseling.

Dr. Gary Collins, professor of psychology and chairman of the Division of Pastoral Psychology and Counseling at Trinity Evangelical Divinity School, has written a unique book called *How to Be a People Helper*.

This book is designed to train lay counselors in the church. Dr. Collins maintains that paraprofessionals, people with some basic training in the areas of counseling and mental health, can be very effective in helping people cope with problems. This is an important concept. Let's be encouraged—trained laymen can touch many lives. Trained lay people have everyday chances to share biblical principles of marriage with their neighbors, often in crisis situations.

Just a couple of months ago, Sharon, a lady in our church called me. "Wayne," she said, "I need help. The couple across the street—really our best friends in the neighborhood—have split up. The husband left three weeks ago. I can't believe it. We thought they had a good marriage. She is terribly depressed and looking to me for help. What should I do?"

I gave the book *How to Be a People Helper* to Sharon and told her to read the chapter on crisis immediately—and then the rest of the book as soon as she could.

I couldn't help thinking about how many similar circumstances happen to Christians every day. These are the kind of times when Christians have a unique opportunity to minister.

Because of that, in our church we are now planning to expand the use of Collins' book *How to Be a People Helper* by training five couples (with the small group approach) in the ministry of "people helping." In addition to the book we will be using the accompanying workbook and training tapes produced by the publisher.

In this training, we also plan to use material from H. Norman Wright's curriculum, *Training Christians to Counsel.* I feel that you can form an effective army of "people helpers" in your church with the use of these two resources.

I also suggest that you investigate local training opportunities for those involved in Christian counseling. Often hospitals and counseling centers have training programs especially for pastors and church staff. Some Bible colleges and seminaries have extension courses that offer help in the skill of counseling.

## Marriage Enrichment Education

Strong, growing marriages just don't happen. Couples must be motivated to place a high priority on their marriage relationship. Often they need specific help on how to have a growing marriage. The concept of the "growing marriage" needs to be continually emphasized. Practical, ongoing marriage enrichment training programs can nurture this growth. Here are some ideas for you to consider.

*Marriage enrichment retreat.* I believe that every church should consider a yearly two-day marriage enrichment retreat for married couples. I have found these retreats one of the finest ways to help strengthen marriages. Couples are able to concentrate on their marriage because the normal distractions— children, to do lists, phone calls, appointments and such are left behind. In the relaxed retreat atmosphere couples seem highly motivated to work diligently together to strengthen their marriages.

You don't have to be a family ministry genius to conduct a marriage enrichment retreat for your church. Good resources are available to help you. For example, I have used the "Growing Marriage" section of H. Norman Wright's handbook *The Christian Faces . . . Emotions, Marriage and Family Relationships.* It is simple to use and very effective. Many of the activities are designed to encourage personal communication between husbands and wives.

Another resource that has been helpful to me is Wright's tape "Conducting Marriage Seminars" which is included in his counseling training resource, *Volume 2—Marriage and Family Counseling.*

In your area, you may have capable people who will conduct marriage enrichment retreats for your church. Keep a lookout for these people. Outside speakers, although not essential, can spark interest in family topics and add a new dimension to your family ministry.

*Sunday School electives.* You can strengthen the family ministry of your church by dedicating one quarter of your Sunday School adult level classes to building the Christian family. There are many paperback books that make good family elective courses. Some have leader's guides that are very helpful for the teacher. For example: *Communication: Key to Your Marriage*, H. Norman Wright—this is a study course with a teacher's guide; *The Christian Couple*, Larry and Nordis Christenson; *What Wives Wish Their Husbands Knew About Women*, James Dobson; *What Every Woman Should Know About a Man*, James L. Johnson; *Dare to Lead*, Timothy Foster—a leader's guide is available; *Tough and Tender*, Joyce Landorf; *Maximum Marriage*, Tim Timmons; *Thoroughly Married*, Dennis Guernsey.

An interesting approach for a marriage elective course is to have separate classes for men and women for three or four weeks and then have the two groups meet together to share with one another insights they have gained. For such an elective, have the men study Dobson's *What Wives Wish Their Husbands Knew About Women*. Have the women use the book by Johnson *What Every Woman Should Know About a Man*.

For another type of elective, use J. Allan Petersen's *Two Become One*. This is a workbook paperback that thoughtfully covers the basic scriptural principles for marriage.

*Seminar courses.* I have found that people respond well to classes offered in a seminar course format; for example, a seminar with classes Thursday night, Friday night and all day Saturday. People who will not commit themselves to a longer course will enroll in a short intensified study.

There are some fine materials designed specifically for seminars.

Lyman Coleman's short course for marriage enrichment, "Evening for Couples," stresses interaction between husbands and wives and is structured to use in four evenings.

Another seminar resource is *Communication and Conflict Resolution in Marriage* by H. Norman Wright. This is a multimedia seminar length course. It includes three sample schedules: an overnight conference; a retreat; and a one-day conference.

Other material can be adapted to fit the seminar approach. I find *Caring Enough to Confront* by David Augsburger is a good book to use in a seminar situation.

In fact, most of the books mentioned in this chapter

can be effectively used in a series of seminar study groups. Experiment with various schedules. Find combinations that fit the needs of your people.

*Family vacation Bible school.* We find that family evening VBS is an excellent opportunity to offer short family related courses. Our evening VBS runs from 7:00 to 9:00 P.M. five consecutive nights so the entire family can attend. This year we offered four adult electives. There were two family topics: "Communicating Christian Values in the Home," and "Building Self-Esteem in Your Family [mainly husband-wife] Through Communication." Persons working on the VBS staff were asked to teach in the children's program for only one hour. This gave everyone a chance to take at least one elective. People who were not involved in the teaching could choose two electives.

*Small groups.* Another way to enrich marriages is through small study groups. Three to five couples can meet for a specific amount of time for the purpose of input, sharing and discussion. I have found a good resource for the small study group approach is *Cherishable: Love and Marriage* by David Augsburger. This study resource includes a paperback book, small group leader's guide, and two cassettes to use during 13 study sessions. The guide has step-by-step procedures for small group sharing and husband and wife dialogue for each of the 13 sessions. For those who have never led nor been a part of a small group the *Cherishable: Love and Marriage* package is a good way to start.

Another way to organize a small group marriage enrichment experience is to have three to five couples meet weekly for a number of weeks to discuss a book on marriage relationships. Each couple should read an assigned chapter before attending the meeting. *The Christian Couple* by Larry and Nordis Christenson is an excellent book for this type of small group. Couples share insights or questions from the book in addition to joys and frustrations of their own marriages. In small groups couples can find great strength as they share, encourage and are encouraged by other caring couples.

*Marriage enrichment dessert.* Sometimes our family education needs a touch of class and elegance (also fun!). A well-done marriage enrichment dessert can be delightful. A church could do this quarterly.

Choose a theme such as "Communicating Love in Marriage." Decorations based on the theme add to the atmosphere. Serve an attractive dessert. Plan activities that emphasize the theme in a meaningful way. The following ideas would add meaning to the theme "Communicating Love in Marriage."

• Ask each person to come prepared to share one creative way to communicate love. (Something like—surprise notes in a shirt pocket or helping with kitchen cleanup without being asked.)

• Encourage husbands and wives to communicate a bit of love and appreciation by giving everyone paper and pencil. Ask each person to write a three-sentence love note to his/her spouse. Then enjoy a few minutes of "communicating love" as couples exchange their notes or read them to one another.

• Select a well-qualified speaker who will give practical suggestions on communicating love in marriage.

• Have a few minutes for silent planning when each person can decide on new ways he/she wants to communicate love during the next week or month.

• Gather a group of interested persons and brainstorm ideas for your marriage enrichment dessert.

*One-night classes:* I have found that an occasional one-night class on a particular topic can be helpful. For example, a few months ago we conducted a one-night class on "Ending Blame in Marriage." We used a chapter from *Caring Enough to Confront* by David Augsburger, as a primary resource. Many books have specific chapters that make good material for a one-night class. For example, chapter 3 of my book, *Getting Your Family Together*, has specific and challenging ideas that will work well for a one-night class. This chapter shows couples, step-by-step, how to have a weekly husband-wife sharing devotional time.

Another approach for the one-night class would be to have couples read a particular book before attending. Persons could then share and summarize the highlights of the book. One of the advantages of this approach is that men, who are noted for their lack of reading family-oriented books, would be motivated to read. (It is estimated that men buy only 20 percent of the books in Christian bookstores—and many of these men are pastors!)

*Book tables:* A large percentage of Christians seldom if ever go into a Christian bookstore. A book table at church gives these persons an opportunity to buy good books on marriage and the family. I really feel that couples who read several good books on marriage relationships each year are nurturing a healthy, growing marriage.

Check with your local Christian bookstore and see if the management will let you have books on consignment. Many will. Review the books carefully and choose the ones you feel will help couples have a growing marriage. Many Christian booksellers will help you arrange a book display for a special family education project.

*Growing marriage fellowship:* Start a "Growing Marriage Fellowship" with a group of couples who are willing to commit themselves to the discipline and hard work of nurturing a growing marriage. Work with the couples to establish requirements for the group. Consider the following ideas:

- Each couple attend one class on marriage relationships each year.
- Each couple have a weekly husband-wife sharing time—a "date."
- Each couple read four required books on marriage each year and attend the follow-up sessions.

Of course, you will want to create your own requirements for such a group. The above ideas are only to start you thinking. The advantage for such a fellowship is that each couple will feel that there is a plan, a direction to their marriage enrichment education—that they have specific goals. Many times family and Christian education in the church lacks this *definite* element. It's a good feeling to have a visual plan with specific, measurable, accomplishment in sight.

Encourage each couple to start a notebook called "Our Growing Marriage Notebook." Resources, together-time notes, records of progress and notes from marriage enrichment courses can be inserted in the notebook. Plan for the family life committee to make periodic mailings of marriage enrichment resources for couples to place in their notebooks. Again, this would be something visual—something to remind them of their commitment.

*Sermon dialogue:* A series of sermons on marriage relationships can be effective, especially if they are thoroughly biblical and highly practical. Some people seem to be interested only in Sunday morning worship. For these people the only marriage enrichment education they may receive will be through these sermons.

To increase the effectiveness of the sermon I suggest a follow-up dialogue session. This could be immediately following the sermon, later in the afternoon or in the evening. The purpose of this dialogue session would be to further clarify and apply the principles presented in the sermon. I suggest that the pastor lead a large group session and then divide persons into smaller groups for discussion and sharing. There are many creative ways in which this kind of dialogue situation can be handled.

*Marriage emphasis week or month:* We have special days, weeks and events to commemorate many things of importance. What is more important than God's first institution, marriage? What would happen in our churches if we set aside a week or month for marriage enrichment each year?

This would say to our people, to God and to our community that we are deeply committed to the sacredness and permanency of marriage. What could be done during this week—or month? Here are some ideas to start you thinking:

• Present a series of special sermons on marriage.

• Bring in special speakers for a week for a marriage seminar.

• Have adult classes conduct a special series of marriage enrichment classes.

• Feature book on marriage each week at a book table in a prominent spot in the church.

• Plan a special service where couples who desire can retake their marriage vows.

• Honor long and successful marriages in your church. Have the couples tell why they believe their marriages have been successful.

• Use creative promotion. Have families work together to make posters illustrating Scriptures on marriage. Place these posters around the church. You might even want to make this a poster contest.

• Conclude your marriage enrichment emphasis time

with a marriage retreat. Note: The first year you have a marriage emphasis week (or month) keep things quite simple. It is best to start small and then expand as God blesses.

*Model a growing marriage:* It is vitally important that the church staff members model a growing marriage. Again, people learn much about family relationships by observing people they admire. The pastor, elders, deacons and teachers should all work toward having healthy, growing marriages. This may be the greatest marriage enrichment training your church could offer.

## You Can Start Now

• Start your own personal library of books to build Christian marriages. (Buy and read at least one a month this year.)

• Start with yourself. Become a people helper. Read *How to Be a People Helper* by Gary Collins.

• Write down two ideas that you will use this year in your church to help couples have growing marriages.

• If you have a family life committee, spend several sessions discussing what your church can do to strengthen marriages. If not, gather a group of interested persons together to plan for marriage enrichment opportunities in your church.

• Note: for additional information on the resources mentioned in this chapter see "Resources for Strengthening Husband-Wife Relationships" following "Reflect and Respond."

## Reflect and Respond

1. Premarital counseling, marriage counseling, and marriage enrichment education are mentioned by the author as major areas in which a church needs to strengthen marriages. On a scale of 1 (the lowest) to 10

(the highest) how would you rate your church's effectiveness in each of these areas?

Premarital Counseling       1 2 3 4 5 6 7 8 9 10
Marriage Counseling        1 2 3 4 5 6 7 8 9 10
Marriage Enrichment       1 2 3 4 5 6 7 8 9 10

2. Which of the three areas mentioned above do you feel is most important for your church to emphasize now?

3. Many ideas for marriage enrichment are given in this chapter. Choose and list several ideas you think would be especially good for your church.

4. The author suggests a marriage emphasis week or month. List three or four possible benefits of such an emphasis.

---

**Note**

1. H. Norman Wright, *Premarital Counseling* (Chicago: Moody Press, 1977) p. 37.

# 6

# Encouraging Healthy Family Relationships

Family relationships are what family life is all about. In this chapter we will talk about just a few of the key aspects of relationships in the family—and what the church can do to strengthen those relationships.

## Parent-Child Relationships

Think for a moment about the day your first child was born. Do you remember the excitement, the pride, the hope, and the fears? When Heidi was a tiny baby my wife and I asked ourselves many times, "Are we doing things right?" I can remember placing Heidi's crib just inches away from our bed. Those first few nights we checked her frequently to see if she was still breathing.

As time went on, we traded in those early fears for other dilemmas: how to toilet train; how to discipline; and in general how to have a good relationship with our precious child. We had little training for our new role as parents. Much was done by trial and error.

We now have three children and Heidi is 12. We are

91

happy with our family. Our commitment to have good relationships with our children has paid off.

However, we would have liked help in those early years. But where were we to receive training to become effective parents? The churches to which we belonged didn't offer such training. My college and seminary training helped little. In fact, the first training on parent-child relationships I participated in was when I was 35. It was a seminar I conducted after being deeply convicted that the church needed to train parents.

Today I feel more convinced than ever that the church has a responsibility to equip parents. We the church are in a unique position to train couples even before they have children. And I am excited about the desire of parents, especially young parents, to be trained in Christian principles of family life. With parents wanting help and with the growing number of excellent resources available, we must offer comprehensive training in parent-child relationships.

*Discipline:* Discipline is a dilemma to many parents. "With so many philosophies and books on the subject, which should I follow?" they ask.

The Bible offers the solution. Parents do not have to "theory hop." Dr. Bruce Narramore in his excellent book, *Help, I'm a Parent!*, combines biblical principles with sound psychology. I suggest that every church use this book as a basic course offered each year to parents. Another excellent book that all parents should read is *Dare to Discipline* by Dr. James Dobson.

Either or both of these books can be used as Sunday School electives. Another idea is to use these books as a basis for a Thursday night, Friday night and Saturday seminar on discipline.

I find that the small group discussion approach works well as a method to train parents in child discipline. Try forming a small group of five or six couples. Schedule meetings for one to two hours one evening a week for 13 weeks. There are numerous books and study courses available to choose from, for example: *Your Child* by Anna B. Mow; *You and Your Child* by Charles Swindoll; and *You Can Have a Happier Family* by Norm Wakefield. (Wakefield's book has a study guide.) Encourage parents to come to each meeting prepared to share their thoughts on an assigned chapter. Discussion and sharing centers on the topic of the evening.

To emphasize the importance of Christian discipline in the home, each year plan to feature "The Book of the Year," on discipline. This book should be carefully selected by the family life committee. Publicize the book in your church bulletin. Suggest that every family with children at home read this book. Hold a follow-up discussion session inviting all those who have read the book. Arrange with the pastor to preach a sermon on "Discipline in the Home." He could promote "The Book of the Year" at this time. Make sure to have the book available for parents to buy or to borrow from the church library.

You may also wish to invite a well-qualified person to speak on child discipline. Many marriage and family counselors do a good job on this topic.

*Self-esteem:* Building self-esteem in children is a major task of all parents. A positive self-image is an important key to our children's success. Most parents feel a need to polish their skills in this area.

There are several resources you can use to help parents have a better understanding of how to build self-esteem. Dr. James Dobson's book, *Hide or Seek*, gives parents good insights into the subject. Dorothy Corkille Briggs has written a very helpful book. Her book, *Your Child's Self-Esteem*, gives practical techniques parents can use every day to build a positive self-image in their children. (Her chapters on discipline, however, tend to lean toward permissiveness.)

I have found that much can be accomplished in parent groups in a short time slot, say in a parent-discussion group working together for two to four hours. Many times I have included discussion on building self-esteem in seminar sessions on discipline or creative parenthood. One excellent resource is *Building Self-Esteem in the Family* by Norm Wakefield. This is a multimedia kit designed to be used in short session. I find that the total content takes less than four hours to present.

Dr. James Dobson contends that adolescence can tear down a child's self-esteem. He has developed an excellent cassette resource to help parents prepare their children for the shock of adolescence. We have used these tapes with Heidi and are very pleased with the results. *Preparing for Adolescence* contains six tapes with titles such as "I Wish I Were Somebody Else," "Self-Esteem and How to Keep It," and "Something Crazy Is Happening to My Body"—(understanding physical and sexual development.) You simply sit down with your child and listen to these tapes, then discuss them. Heidi has commented, "I sure like Dr. Dobson. He's neat!"

I feel that every church should make these tapes available to their families. To make certain the tapes are used effectively, schedule a training session with parents. Play segments of the tapes and explain how to use them with their children.

*Family unity:* There are few topics so crucial for today's families as building family unity. Let's face it, society and sometimes the church puts so much demand on the family's time that it has little energy left for building loving relationships within the home. This is sad. Families will never be all that God wants them to be until they build close, loving relationships. These kinds of relationships come from spending quality time together—doing constructive, happy things together as a family.

Churches need to be extremely careful that they do nothing to tear down family unity. Whenever your church schedules an event, evaluate it by asking: "How does this affect the entire family?"

Churches need to take positive steps to help homes build family unity. We need to show by our programming that we believe it is important for family members to be together.

For example, by having entire families worship together rather than providing age-graded junior churches the church says: "Families are important!" I realize that this is a loaded subject, but at least give it some thought. I feel strongly that family unity is built when families worship God together. Pastors need to be aware of how they can meet needs of the total family. In my book, *Good Times for Your Family*, I suggest activities that families can do together during the sermon and then share the results at home.[1]

Families can learn together. Last summer I led a three-day family camp that was truly *family*. Entire family units learned together as a family and as extended families in clusters. By doing this, we helped families see the potential of doing things together at home.

I feel it is important for churches to plan times for families to learn together. In my book, *Getting Your Family Together*, I include a section on how churches can plan specific activities for families together at the church.[2]

A Sunday School elective that entire families can take one quarter a year would be a valuable experience. I have not seen a suitable resource for this as yet. However, I find that family night plans, such as are featured in *Family Life Today* magazine can be adapted and used effectively in family groups.

The church can also provide all-family recreation opportunities. At one time I belonged to a church that scheduled a family gym night twice a month during the winter. They were able to use one of the junior high gyms at no cost. A game-recreation evening can be planned for families even if no gym is available.

Our church will be having some family movie nights this year. Good, full-length movies are available at reasonable rates. With the high cost and the extremely poor quality of many movies at theaters, a church can do a real service for families by providing wholesome entertainment with a family movie night at the church.

Encourage your church families to have family potlucks. Four or five families can get together for a good time of fellowship while they eat and play together.

Start collecting recreational resources that families can check out from your church. I know some churches that have backpacking outfits, skis, table games, and a wide assortment of other recreational items that families can borrow and use.

Hobbies and crafts that families do together can build family fun and family unity. Many families, however, need a little help to get started. Why not have a "Family Hobby and Craft Learning Fair" at your church? Select competent people to teach entire families to do such things as decoupage, rock cutting and polishing, flower arranging, fabric painting, and how to make interesting handcrafts. This list could go on and on depending on the skills and interests of your people!

I find there are several good resources to help your families build family unity. The first, *Building Family Unity* by Gladys Hunt, is a multimedia learning kit designed to be used in an overnight conference or retreat setting. A second family unity builder by Gladys Hunt is *Honey for a Child's Heart*. This book should be read by every parent. It is delightful. The book focuses on how to build family unity by reading good books together in the family.

My book, *Getting Your Family Together*, helps families "find family time," by evaluating their schedules. The book contains many activities that families can do together. This book can be used in small groups, as a Sunday School elective, or in family vacation Bible schools. (See chapter 12.)

*You Can Have a Happier Family* by Norm Wakefield is another book that helps families build family unity. This book has a study guide for group use.

A very reasonably priced paperback with a wealth of recreational ideas is Marion Leach Jacobson's book, *How to Keep Your Family Together and Still Have Fun*.

On a family emphasis Sunday, arrange with your Christian bookstore to have a "family togetherness" display of books that will help families build family unity.

## Family Communication

Communication is an essential part of healthy family relationships. Good family relationships improve communication and good communication builds strong family relationships.

One of the best ways to build good communication throughout the entire family is to help couples establish good communication in their marriage. The children learn by the example of their parents how to communicate with others in the family. This is another reason why *strengthening husband and wife relationships* is a key area in the church's ministry to families.

But even when a husband and wife communicate well

in their marriage there is still a need to train the whole family. Here are some resources that will help.

*Family Communication: A Guide to Emotional Health* by clinical psychologist Sven Wahlroos is one of the best resources on the market for understanding key principles of family communication.

H. Norman Wright has written an excellent little book called *An Answer to Family Communication.* This book can be used with small groups or can be given to couples or families to study on their own. Included are communication exercises that family members can do together.

Many parents, when their children reach adolescence, are very motivated to increase their skills in communication. There are some fine resources available to use with parents and teens. A complete parent-teen curriculum called *Building Positive Parent-Teen Relationships* is written by Rex Johnson and H. Norman Wright.

This course is designed to be used with parents and teens together. It can also be adapted to be taught to teens or parents separately. The manual contains: 24 hours of actual instructional content; 12 full-color transparencies; 12 ready-made duplicating masters. I have used this material in a parent-teen seminar and I recommend it highly.

A series of cassette tapes, *Parent-Teen Relationships*, prepared by H. Norman Wright provides listening and discussion material for parents and their teenagers. These tapes deal with many of the sticky problems faced by parents and teens.

### Single Adults

"The people of God are on the edge of one of the greatest adventures the church has ever known. We are beginning to see all persons—particularly the divorced, widowed, and single adults—in our midst. Ministry with and to them is the church's new frontier." This statement by Britton Wood, single adult minister of the Park Cities Baptist Church in Dallas, Texas reflects the feelings of many Christians. The church has a great opportunity in ministering to both the formerly married and the unmarried.

You can start a ministry to singles whether you have 1 or 100 singles in your church. Any church can meet a single person's need for acceptance understanding and someone to really care for them.

When I first met with the singles in a church where I was the new minister of family life I received a shock. During that meeting a young lady said, "We thought you would never notice us. It seems like this church doesn't know we exist."

I'm afraid that this has been true not only of that church but many churches in the past. We must minister to everyone—including groups such as the singles—who have special needs. Just reaching out to meet a few of their needs, just letting them know that we are conscious they are there, says to the singles that we care.

To determine the needs of the singles in our church we had several meetings. At one meeting I had each single adult make a four-column list with the words shown below at the head of each column.

| Social | Mental | Spiritual | Physical |
|--------|--------|-----------|----------|
|        |        |           |          |
|        |        |           |          |
|        |        |           |          |
|        |        |           |          |

I asked everyone to write what he felt his needs were in those areas. Then on a separate sheet of paper I had each person write what he felt the singles and the church together could do to meet those needs. We combined lists and came up with a comprehensive view of the needs of the group along with suggestions for action.

There is a growing number of resources available to help meet the needs of singles in our churches. Many churches have successful ministries to singles. Their ideas can help us get started. The periodical *Solo* published by the Garden Grove Community Church, in Garden Grove, California, gives many ideas and insights to encourage and bolster singles' groups.

Dr. Charles Edward Smith of Encino, California has formed the California organization of "One-Parent Families." Dr. Smith will send information if you write him and enclose a self-addressed envelope. For $1.00 this organization has a questionnaire designed to increase awareness of needs both for the one-parent family and for your family life committee. (One-Parent Families, 16255 Ventura Blvd., Encino, CA. 91426.)

The singles in your church will appreciate a special section of books in the church library for singles and single parents. Virginia Watts' book, *The Single Parent*, is a valuable book for the solo-parent and it includes a useful listing of other resources. Also, the listing of resources for singles at the end of this chapter will give you additional suggestions for books to add to your church library.

Raising children without a spouse is a difficult task. Yet a large and growing number of single parents face this reality. The church needs to provide opportunities for single parents to get together so they can share problems, as well as encourage one another. I have found in my seminars that some of the most receptive and appreciative people are the single parents. Often they are seeking help on how to build a Christian home and develop a Christian life-style.

The church needs to explore many possible ways for providing fellowship for singles and single-parent families. For example:

• One church in California has a potluck meal after the Sunday morning service where two-parent and single-parent families gather for a good time of fellowship. This is a fine way to help the single-parent child enjoy the companionship of other children and to have the opportunity to get acquainted with their parents.

• Men teaching in the preschool and children's divisions of the Sunday School can help youngsters living with their mothers experience a man's influence. Note: Singles are often excellent teachers.

• If you have too few singles in your church to start a fellowship group, contact other churches and singles' groups in your area. Many churches are meeting the needs of their singles by forming interdenominational Christian singles' groups.

• Many people in the church are unaware of the viewpoint of singles. Why not plan an evening service with a panel comprised of singles? Encourage the people on the panel to speak positively and frankly about their "single experience" as they talk about advantages of the Christian single life as well as the needs of the single person. Include a time for questions and discussion.

• One pastor I know has a luncheon periodically where the widows of the church can come together for a time of sharing and fellowship. Such occasions give alert members of the church staff opportunities to observe needs and to get acquainted with individuals who are eager to find places of service in the church.

• I am aware of two resources that are designed to be

101

used with singles in a retreat or seminar setting. *Developing a Positive Single Identity* and *Beginning Again: The Challenge of the Formerly Married* are both multimedia learning kits. Each kit provides a complete plan for a retreat.

## Middle Age

In many churches the people in their middle years are looked upon as "pillars of the church." Pillars or not, the middle-agers have their own set of struggles. Two major questions that face them are: "How do we adjust when all of our children have left home?" and "How should we prepare for retirement?"

How are you helping the middle-aged people in your congregation answer these questions? Are you aware of other questions they may be asking?

Assign two or three members of your family life committee to come up with suggestions for specific ways your church can minister more effectively to the middle-age group. For example: add books to the church library that deal with "the empty nest" and retirement; plan a retreat for the "Over-Fifty Under Sixty-Fivers"; plan an evening service where older people can share how they faced "the empty nest" and some of their retirement experiences.

## Older People

One Sunday shortly after starting as family life minister at the church in Beaverton, Oregon, I preached a sermon on the family. After the sermon one of the ushers brought me a note. It simply said, "You did not mention grandparents. Are they no longer part of the family?"

At first I was defensive. I thought "In this sermon it was not appropriate to mention grandparents."

But the more I reflected on that note, the more I began to feel the person who wrote it had great insight. What have we done with our older people? Are churches going along with society and putting the oldsters out to pasture at age 65? In what significant ways do we make these persons feel important? Useful? Loved?

This episode motivated us to have a special day to honor the older people in our congregation. We called it "Grandparents Day." I wish we could make this a national holiday. We honor mothers and fathers—why not grandparents?

On Grandparents Day I preached a special sermon on the value of grandparents and all older people. We gave carnations to all those over 60 and gifts to the grandparents who were the oldest, youngest and to grandparents with the most grandchildren and great grandchildren.

We asked the younger families in our congregation to invite the older ones to dinner. This worked out great. A few days later one young couple called me and said, "Thanks, Wayne, for the opportunity of getting to know the Martins. Did you know that they were pioneers in this area? We had a delightful time."

In our churches we must work diligently to bring the old and the young together. Older persons have so much to share with younger persons. But this sharing will never happen unless we specifically plan to bring the generations together.

Unfortunately, we have bought society's line that it is always better to separate people into age groups. Often I feel we have been sold a mess of pottage! This is the very thing that causes generation gaps and deprives younger people of the great wisdom of life that can only be shared by older people.

There are various ways in which persons of all ages can be brought together. I have already mentioned the merit of occasional all-family groupings in the Sunday School. If you have a closely graded adult Sunday School division you can profitably mix the classes one Sunday a quarter. If you have electives you probably already have a wide spread of ages in each class.

In Napa, California, at a church where I was on the staff, the young people planned a social for our senior citizens. They did the whole thing from planning the dessert, to serving and providing the entire program. This was a highlight of the year for both the youth and the senior citizens!

Many churches are seeing the great potential of working with their older members and are organizing fine senior citizen ministries. Trips are planned. Socials are held. Older people are encouraged to use their wisdom and skills to serve in the church. Older people are recognized for their strength as "prayer warriors." Some churches are hiring special staff persons to minister to the needs of older persons in the church and develop opportunities for service.

The potential is unlimited—both in meeting the needs of senior citizens and in helping them share their lives in a useful way with others.

### This Is Just a Beginning

We have certainly not exhausted the extent of family relationships that need to be strengthened. There are also many fine resources available that I have not mentioned. I have tried to share with you the ones I have found useful. The manual, *Family Ministries in Your Church* by Sheldon Louthan and Grant Martin, suggests a wealth of family ministry resources. Also, the Christian Marriage Enrichment *Marriage and Family Resource Newsletter* is an excellent source of ideas for materials.

I want to emphasize that the areas in which you choose to encourage healthy family relationships in your church families will depend on the needs of your people. The "Family Life Questionnaire" in chapter 2 of this book will help you determine those needs.

## You Can Start Now

• If you haven't already done so, administer the Family Life Questionnaire in chapter 2 of this book and determine family relationship needs of families in your congregation.

• Make a plan to purchase needed resources that will help families discover how they can improve relationships in their homes.

• Decide on a time and resource for a class on discipline in the family.

• List two ideas you have found in this chapter that you feel your family life committee should attempt during the coming year.

• Note: For additional information on the resources mentioned in this chapter see "Resources for Encouraging Healthy Family Relationships" following "Reflect and Respond."

## Reflect and Respond

1. What do you feel are the basic areas in which parents in your church most need to be trained? List at least two areas.

2. The author states that family unity is extremely important. Do you agree? What effects do you see that

family unity, or the lack of it is having on your church? Your church families?

3. List the times when families in your church get together as entire families at the church.

4. Draw up, in rough outline form, a tentative plan for encouraging healthy family relations in your church families. Be specific.

---

**Notes**

1. Wayne E. Rickerson, *Good Times for Your Family* (Glendale, CA: Regal Books, 1976), p. 95.
2. Wayne E. Rickerson, *Getting Your Family Together* (Glendale, CA: Regal Books, 1976). See chapter 12.

# 7
# Enabling Parents to Teach Christian Values

The children of Israel were knocking at the door of the Promised Land after years of wandering. God, through Moses, gave parents some final instructions on how they were to teach scriptural values to their children in the new land.

*Hear, O Israel! The Lord is our God, the Lord is one! And you shall love the Lord your God with all your heart and with all your soul and with all your might. And these words, which I am commanding you today, shall be on your heart; and you shall teach them diligently to your sons and shall talk of them when you sit in your house and when you walk by the way and when you lie down and when you rise up. And you shall bind them as a sign on your hand and they shall be as frontals on your forehead. And you shall write them on the doorposts of your house and on your gates (Deut. 6:4-9).*

Note that *three* basic principles of teaching were given. First, parents were to teach by their example. They were to love the Lord wholeheartedly. God's words were to be on the parents' hearts first.

Second, they were to take God's commands seriously and "teach them diligently" to their children. This phrase suggests a structured teaching situation, a time set aside by parents to share God's Word with their young people.

Third, Hebrew parents were also to use informal situations to teach God's value to their children. They were to "talk" as they sat in the house, as they lay down, as they got up, and as they walked.

The whole future of the nation of Israel rested on how well the parents carried out God's instructions. When the parents taught this way, the next generation followed God. When the principles were violated, the next generation worshiped idols. We see many examples of this in the Old Testament.

Throughout the entire Bible God always places the responsibility for teaching Christian values to children on the parents. God has always intended for parents to be the primary communicators of values to their children.

## What About Christian Parents Today?

Do Christian parents today feel responsible for the Christian education of their children? Do they, in fact, teach Christian values to their children?

Of course, parents always teach values in the home. This is unavoidable. But what I am asking is: Do parents *consciously* teach Christian values to their children? Do they work at being a good example? Do they look for the informal times to share Bible teachings and Christian values? Do they take time to read and discuss Scripture in the home?

I am coming to feel that the majority of parents do not consciously teach Christian values to their children. Most parents feel that the church is primarily responsible for teaching the meaning of Christianity to children.

With Scripture so clear on the topic why is there so little planned teaching going on in Christian homes today? At least part of the answer is given, I feel, by Anna B. Mow in her book, *Your Child.* She says:

> *The late Dr. C.C. Ellis of Juniata College wondered why some of the devout Christian leaders of the last century should have objected to the Sunday School movement. Why did they object to the church teaching religion to children? Alert scholar that he was, he went to the archives of old Eastern Pennsylvania churches to find what reasons they gave in their council meeting minutes for such objections. To his astonishment it was not that they were reluctant to take on something new. Instead he found their recorded objection to be: "If the church takes up the teaching of the children, the homes will let it go and will leave the responsibility to the church!" How discerning the old brethren were! That is exactly what has happened.[1]*

Over a period of years the church has become more and more involved in the Christian education of children while the parents have taken a back seat. It is not necessary to make a judgment as to who is at fault. But we do need to recognize that the problem exists and take steps to solve it.

I am *not* saying that we should throw out the educational programs of the church. Our children need to have teachers—adult models—other than their parents. And children need to be together with their own Christian peer group. The question is *how can the educational program of the church and the home work together.*

We must answer the questions: What is the responsibility of the church? What is the responsibility of the home?

The church has a fundamental responsibility in the Christian education of children. However, that responsibility is not primarily to teach children but to equip parents to teach *their own* children. This will mean a major shift of emphasis in our current church educational systems.

Diagram 1 shows a typical church-centered Christian educational program.

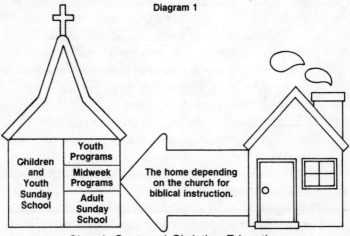

Diagram 1

Church-Centered Christian Education

In Diagram 2 we have a family ministry alternative. The major emphasis is on equipping adults, a strong New Testament educational concept, which is brought

110

into sharp focus in Ephesians 4:1-16. A major function of this family alternative is to equip adults to teach biblical principles to their own children.

When this happens, the home will feed back into the church's educational program parents who are well qualified to teach there because they have been teaching their own children at home. Children and youth will be stronger assets to the church educational programs because they will have been taught and disciplined at home. The potential for children's and youth programs will be infinite.

Diagram 2

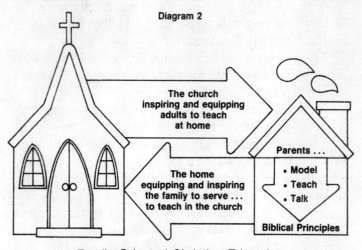

Family-Oriented Christian Education

If the primary function of the church is to equip parents to teach Christian values to their children and to be teachers in the church, then we as church leaders must make some major changes in our educational emphasis.

First, our adult educational programs need to have the *number one priority*. The very best resources and training should be used to equip adults. A central part of this training needs to include enabling parents to teach Christian values to their children at home.

Since, according to Scripture, parents are primarily responsible for teaching values to their children, they need as much, if not more, training and resources than do those who teach in our Sunday Schools. Most churches I know, even the ones who say they believe parents have key responsibility for teaching their children, offer little, if any help for the parents.

Not long ago I was discussing this problem with a Christian education director who is committed to equipping families for Christian teaching. "Jerry," I asked, "how much does your church spend on materials for parents' training compared to the budget for church-centered Christian education?"

"Five thousand for the Sunday School and youth programs and one hundred for our family program," was his reply. "It's sad, isn't it?"

Of course, that $5,000 for Christian education materials is helping family members learn more about their faith. But we must be giving parents more direct help. You see, most of us have a long way to go. We may say we believe in parents teaching their children, but our actions say something else.

However, if church leaders do want to match their Sunday School budget with an equal amount for resources and training for parents, where can they buy materials? Fortunately, there is a growing number of family education resources available. For information see "Resources for Enabling Parents to Teach Christian Values" at the end of this chapter.

### Our Great Old Frontier

We are on the threshold of a great—not new—old frontier. This old frontier we have to conquer is to enable parents to return to being the primary teachers of the basic Christian values to their own children.

I have some suggestions on how we can make this happen. First, the biblical philosophy that parents are primarily responsible to teach their children must be accepted by the leadership of the church. By "accepted" I do not mean a weak acknowledgement that "the Bible does say that, but it is very idealistic." That parents are responsible to teach Christian values to their children should be a building block philosophy of the church. It may take 20 years to see this goal accomplished but the church leadership should commit themselves to see it happen.

The philosophy should be understood and lived out by all church leadership. Sunday School teachers and youth program directors should constantly remind parents by both word and action that, "We want to equip you to teach your family Christian truth every day in the home."

We should avoid sending contradictory messages to parents. If we say that parents are primarily responsible to teach their children and then conduct only church-centered children's programs without directly involving parents we contradict ourselves. If God says that parents are responsible to teach their own children, *are they not just as responsible to teach them in the programs of the church as they are at home?* I believe they are.

In Napa, California where I was director of Christian education, the elders passed a motion stating that the educational philosophy of the church was that parents were responsible for the Christian education of their own children. Since then, the church has persistently pressed in that direction. Parents are equipped to teach at home. *They are also expected to teach in the Sunday School and youth groups of the church!*

Many churches have a difficult time recruiting Sunday School teachers and youth workers. Perhaps, it is because we are not doing things God's way. Why not recruit parents of children and young people for our Sunday School teachers and youth leaders?

Wherever I have worked as a family life minister and/or Christian education director I have always made it a practice to participate in church-centered educational programs for our children. Heidi is now in junior high. This year my wife Janet and I volunteered to be youth sponsors. In fact, we have four couples all with junior high children who *wanted* to serve as sponsors. We all feel responsible for the Christian education of our children. As a result we have the most vital, growing junior high youth program this church has ever seen.

## Family Nights

Have you ever wondered how the Mormons are able to have so many parents committed to teaching in the home? One Mormon elder told me that 90 percent of active Mormon families have regular family nights. It is because home-centered religious education is a building block philosophy of the Mormon church. Monday nights are reserved by the Mormon people as a time for parents to teach principles of their faith at home. An outstanding *Family Home Evening Manual* is given to parents every year. *In front of each manual is a message from the president of the Mormon church reminding parents how essential it is for them to teach at home.*

How can we train parents in our churches to teach at home? Let me share with you some ideas and resources.

I feel that the best way to get parents started teaching in the home is to help them start family nights—regular family together times. These are informal, fun, once a week family times based on God's Word. Parents get a taste of success through family nights and then are open to other kinds of family teaching. Informal teaching and teaching by example seem to grow out of the consciousness raised by dedicating one night a week to sharing together as a family.

The church should encourage at-home family nights by designating one night a week as "Family Night." Families should be encouraged to spend this night at home. No church-related activities should be scheduled for that night.

*Family Life Today* magazine, published by Gospel Light Publications, contains a section called "Family Time Ideas." There are four complete family time plans in each monthly issue. I suggest that all parents of a church receive a copy of this valuable magazine every month.

I conduct "Creative Home Teaching Seminars" to help churches train their parents on how to teach Christian values at home. In this eight-hour seminar parents learn such things as: how to have successful family nights; how to use the dinner hour effectively; how to build family unity; and how to have regular family devotions.

I feel one of the best ways to train parents on how to have family nights is to have other families show them how. For example, we have invited a family in our church to join our family for our next family night. We will simply include them in our activities. The parents will see how a family night is handled. After dessert I will explain in more detail to the parents how to conduct a family night and give them resource materials. I will then follow this initial training session with encouragement and more resources.

In our church we have a lay couple who is in charge of developing our family night ministry. They frequently have families into their home for training and they schedule other family night trainers. They also keep a record of the families in the church who are having regular family nights and frequently share resources and ideas.

Parents must have steady encouragement and resources if they are to continue family nights. The dropout rate is quite high if either support or resources are not adequate.

In the book *Facing the Future—Church and Family Together*, edited by Gary Collins, I have a chapter titled "Developing Creative Home Teaching." The chapter is designed to be a tool for church leaders to use in training parents how to conduct family nights and how to teach by example and teach informally.

Also, my book, *Getting Your Family Together*, is primarily designed to help church leaders train parents how to teach Christian values at home. Some of the topics covered are: Developing Family Values; Teaching Values by Example; Planning a Regular Family Night; Creating Family Unity at the Dinner Table; Developing Creative Bible Study; Memorizing Scripture Together; and Teaching in Informal Moments. This book focuses on practical ideas parents can use to teach at home. The final chapter of the book provides the church leader with 11 parent enabling sessions to be used in family study groups, family vacation Bible school, or Sunday School classes.

Another one of my books, *Good Times for Your Family*, contains over 100 ideas for creative family times based on God's Word.

Two books with family night material have been written by Lois Bock and Miji Working: *Happiness Is a Family Time Together* and *Happiness Is a Family Walk with God*, both contain ideas for family nights. *How to Keep the Family That Prays Together from Falling Apart* by Elva Anson is also loaded with good suggestions for family nights and other family time teaching experiences.

## Family Enabling Sessions

As minister of family life at the Christian Church in Beaverton, Oregon I have developed what we call "Family Enabling Nights." This night is designed to equip parents to teach Christian values at home. It is also a time when entire families get together for learning and fellowship.

We have a family enabling night every other month. Complete families, babies through teenagers, arrive at the church at 7:00 P.M. for a time of sharing. We start the evening by grouping three to five families together in family clusters. We then give them an activity to do together. That takes about 20-30 minutes.

After the family cluster activity, the children see a movie or have recreation while parents meet for specific training that we call "Parent Enabling." This one hour session is broken into sharing, input and planning. During this time we provide training and resources to enable parents to have successful family times. A major feature is material for family nights.

To conclude the evening, families come back together for a time of fellowship and food. Often, each family brings a dessert to share.

In my book, *Getting Your Family Together*, I have included a special section with complete plans for 11 family enabling nights—one session for each chapter in the book.

## Family Cluster Education

At the present time there is a growing interest in family cluster education—that is, entire families and individuals learning together in groups of 15-20 people. This type of education can help parents learn how to have effective Bible learning times at home. Family clusters are effective when the cluster leader models for other parents how all ages can learn together. For example, in a family cluster situation a father who is quite intimidated by the whole family teaching concept, can watch another father lead families in enjoyable activities. Quite often, after observing, the hesitant father thinks, "That doesn't look so hard. I could do that with my own family."

I do not feel that a total family cluster approach will ever replace the traditional Sunday School. There are valid reasons for children and parents to have learning times apart from one another. We need to remember that the greatest task of the educational program of the church *is to equip adults for ministry.*

Family clusters do have a place in our educational programs but should not dominate our thinking. If we focus on church programs such as family clustering, then learning remains church-centered. If, on the other hand, we concentrate on the importance of teaching and learning in the home we help parents understand their God-assigned role.

Intergenerational learning should be a part of our overall educational program. As I mentioned before, I think churches could offer a "Family Cluster Elective" that family members could take one quarter each year. However, there are many other times that intergenerational learning can occur. Family vacation Bible schools, evening training programs, family camps, or just one evening called "Family Affairs" could be used as times for all ages to learn together.

There is another educational approach that emphasizes the family. This is "Sunday School Plus" developed by Larry Richards. This home-church educational package has a relational, life-focused children's curriculum for Sunday School use. Parents can enroll in the related Sunday School adult elective and study the same material as their children. There is material for parents to use with their children at home that ties into the single theme.

I firmly believe that God rewards the families who take seriously their responsibility to teach Christian values at home. I have seen it in home after home. Families are drawn closer together. Parents grow spiritually. Fathers take steps to become the kind of spiritual leaders that God wants them to be. Family communication increases. Children acquire a real interest in spiritual things and often become strong committed Christians. All of this happens because once again the home becomes what God intended for it to be—a center of Christian education.

**You Can Start Now**

• Ask the leadership of your church to make the biblical principle of: *Parents are primarily responsible to teach Christian values to their children* an official philosophy of the church.

• Set aside a night to train parents on how to have family nights. Use chapter 6 of *Getting Your Family Together*, "Planning a Regular Family Night," to help parents get started. Provide as many resources for parents as you can afford. (See "Resources for Enabling Parents to Teach Christian Values" at the end of this chapter.) Have families who already have family nights give testimonies of what it has done for their families. These families could also give tips on, "What Makes Our Family Nights Successful."

• Use "Family Enabling Sessions" in chapter 12 of

*Getting Your Family Together* with the families in your congregation.

• Encourage your church to set aside one night during the week when families can always depend on being home. No church-related activities should be scheduled for that night.

• Acquaint families in your church with the magazine, *Family Life Today*. Take time to point out features like the "Family Times" section. If your church would like to have free copies of back issues of *Family Life Today* to distribute to your congregation, write to: *Family Life Today*, 110 W. Broadway, Glendale, CA 91204.

• Use study discussion feature articles from *Family Life Today* in parent study groups, Sunday School classes, panel discussions, and retreat study groups.

• Note: For additional information on the resources mentioned in this chapter, see "Resources for Enabling Parents to Teach Christian Values" following "Reflect and Respond."

**Reflect and Respond**

1. Is there evidence in your church that parents feel responsible for the Christian teaching of their own children? How many, would you say, actually do some kind of consistent teaching within the home? How many parents are teaching in your Sunday School, sponsoring youth groups, etc.?

2. Do you agree or disagree with Anna B. Mow that

parents have left the responsibility of teaching Christian values to their children to the church?

3. Do you feel that the author makes a legitimate statement when he says that "parents . . . need as much, if not more, training and resources than do those who teach in our Sunday Schools"? Give some reasons for your answer.

4. Do leaders in your church set an example by: (1) consistently teaching Christian values to their own children in the home? (2) encouraging parents to teach in the Christian education program of the church?

---

**Note**

1. Anna B. Mow, *Your Child* (Grand Rapids: Zondervan Publishing House, 1963), p. 23.

# 8
# Equipping Families
# to Minister
# to Others

What is the most persistant problem in your church? If your church is like many I've known and been a part of, your greatest problem is that a small percentage of the membership is doing most of the work.

What is the reason for this? Is it that people just are not interested in serving God? Or could it be that we haven't given enough thought and action to equipping members of the church for ministry?

Is it possible that we could reverse this trend by equipping families to minister to others? I believe so. Families can be the greatest potential for ministry the church has ever seen.

To begin with, I believe the family is a place to train children to minister. Probably most of you have seen parents and children of certain sects proselyting door to door. The children are not along just because the parents can't find baby-sitters. These sects know the great potential of the family unit to serve the church and also to train children.

Have evangelical Christians overlooked the home as a catalyst for ministry? We put adults to work but often ignore complete families and especially children. We tell our children, if not in word, in action, "Wait. Someday you will be able to serve the Lord." And so they wait and wait. And when they become adults we say, "Now is the time. We want you to serve now." And they say no. We wonder why they are not interested. I'm afraid we haven't trained them well.

One Sunday shortly after we moved to Beaverton, Oregon we were worshiping together as a family in church. Our sixth-grader Heidi was reading the church bulletin. She got my attention and pointed to an announcement that read: "Helper wanted for the four-year-old Sunday School class."

Heidi pointed to herself with a gesture that said, "Could I volunteer, Dad?' '

My heart sank. I was afraid the answer might be, "We just don't let children help in our Sunday School."

Later that day, Heidi asked a rather startled Sunday School superintendent if she could be the helper in that class. Now I don't know whether the Sunday School superintendent was caught off guard or whether it was because it was his wife who was crying for help, but he consented to let Heidi help for a few Sundays.

Sometime later he came to me and confessed, "My wife says Heidi is terrific with the kids. I guess we will let her stay." A year later Heidi is still serving with as much enthusiasm as when she started.

All three of our girls are highly motivated to serve the Lord. It seems to be a natural expression of their faith. Let me share with you some reasons why I think this has occurred. It is basically because we have always served the Lord together as a family. Our children have always felt a part of our ministry and have been given a chance to serve in small ways. (Ways that seem small to adults, that is.)

In my senior year of college we moved to Issaquah, Washington to help start a new church. Our girls helped to set up chairs in the lodge that we used as meeting place. We made many calls together as a family. Our home was the center of activity for this young church.

Then during seminary days we committed ourselves to helping families. Again, the entire family was involved. We started family nights in our home and helped other families do the same. The girls also helped me in many of the Creative Family Teaching seminars.

My first book of family night materials was a family project. The entire family helped put the 128-page loose-leaf manuals together. Again, ministry was a family affair.

Each time our family moves into a new neighborhood we see it as our mission field. We reach out together and make many contacts for Jesus.

Children do not learn to minister by merely watching their parents walk out the door at night to "serve the Lord." Out of sight modeling does not always work. In fact, this many times gives children a negative view of serving God. They see the church as competing for their parents' time. The real training comes when families become involved together in serving God and others.

A family will not become "ingrown" when its focus is on serving others. Some feel that one of the real dangers of a strong family ministry in the church is that families will become "home centered" and forget about everything but building their own family. True, the family can become an excuse for not fellowshipping with other Christians and serving God. But I have found there is no real conflict between building a strong family unity and the family serving others. There needs to be time for the family to be alone and also time to share with others.

Edith Schaeffer expresses this idea beautifully in her book, *What is a Family?*

> When asked *"What is a family?"* and the answer comes *"a door,"* it seems to me the more accurate definition would be, *"A family is a door that has hinges and a lock."* The hinges should be well oiled to swing the door open during certain times, but the lock should be firm enough to let people know that the family needs to be alone part of the time, just to be a family. If a family is to be really shared, then there needs to be something to share. Whatever we share needs time for preparation.[1]

Now for the big question. *How do we equip families to serve others?* It is obvious to me as I write this that not many persons have done creative thinking on this topic. Resources about how to involve families in service are few. This probably says something about our focus within the church—and why we have about 20 percent of the people doing about 80 percent of the work in so many churches.

I believe that *families serving others* needs to be an integral philosophy of the church. We are reborn to serve. This biblical principle needs to be taught, preached and lived out within the leadership of the church.

We also need to help families find opportunities to serve. Although this should be a natural outgrowth of a growing personal relationship with God, it seems to need cultivating.

Use the following ideas to help motivate families in your church to serve others.

### Hospitality

Welcoming others into our homes is a real opportunity for service. God's Word says hospitality is important (see 1 Pet. 4:9). It is even spelled out as a prerequisite for leadership within the church (see 1 Tim. 3:2). But it seems to me that open homes—warm hospitality—have become a thing of the past for many families in our churches.

Karen Mains has written an inspiring book on how to find joy through sharing your home with others. *Open Heart—Open Home* restores biblical hospitality to its proper place for twentieth-century Christian families. I recommend you read this book and then pass it on to others. In fact, this book would make a good resource for small Bible study groups.

Mrs. Mains shares from her own growing experiences of hospitality:

> *Yet, I have discovered that even an innate inclination to hospitality must be honed and refined, imbued and filled, if it is to be more than concern about centerpices, menus, table settings and spotless rooms. For Christians, hospitality is a marvelous gift of the Holy Spirit given so that we may minister to this dying society. If our hospitality is to minister, to impart to each who crosses our threshold something of the presence of Christ—if it is to transcend the human and deal in the supernatural—there must be an agony of growth, a learning, a tutoring at the hand of the Holy Spirit.* [2]

Start a hospitality revolution in your church. Begin with your own home. Disciple others to open their homes to both those inside and outside the church. Recommend that the pastor preach a sermon or a sermon series on Christian hospitality. Have an "Open Home Week" where each family is encouraged to invite at least one other family to share fellowship and food. Feature Mrs. Mains' book in your church library publicity. Encourage family potlucks where two or three families get together. Have families give testimonies of what happened when they opened their homes to others.

Here is an activity that you can give to families in your church that will help them see the need to open up their homes to neighbors. Our family had a lot of fun doing this. First we drew a large map of our neighborhood on a long strip of butcher paper. The children drew in details such as houses, trees, and flowers. Next we took a test to see how much we knew about who lived in the houses within a two-block radius. The questions were: What is the neighbor's full name? What are the names of the children? What is the husband's occupation? What is the family's hobby? Are they Christians? Each family member scored one point for each correct answer. We then totaled the points to see who knew most about our neighbors. (Neither my wife nor myself won!)

We concluded this "hospitality" activity by reading Jesus' teaching to "Love your neighbor as yourself." We discussed that to really love someone we must learn to know them. We then made plans to open our home and to get acquainted with our neighbors.

### Family Evangelism

We train individuals for evangelism, why not families? Through hospitality, families could first build relationships with other families. Then, when God provides the opportunity, families could share their faith naturally in the relaxed friendly atmosphere of the home.

Why not develop a family clinic to train entire families on how to share their faith? Families could be given key Scriptures to memorize during their family nights or other appropriate times. Some families might also choose to use the *Four Spiritual Laws* produced by Campus Crusade. Think of the learning that occurs when children watch their parents lead others to Christ.

## Mission Projects

Many innovative projects can be designed to help families serve others through missions. A project designed by Lud Golz, pastor of fellowship Bible Church in Novelty, Ohio, is an example of what can be done in your church.

Pastor Golz wanted to help parents involve their families in missions. He designed a bank container in the shape of a Bible out of corrugated cardboard. He then made an instruction sheet for everyone in the congregation and challenged families to make a bank and collect money for two months before Christmas. On Christmas Day the banks were collected and the money was sent to "Bibles for the World" with the request that the organization send the Bibles to Russia. Here's an account of what happened.

> *On Christmas Sunday the children proudly brought their banks to church. During the service they came to the front and held their banks for all to see. Then we had all the children go out into the congregation and collect as much as they could from the people, using their banks as the containers. This was one of the few times I have participated in a "hilarious offering." People gave joyfully. Children collected enthusiastically —and the total was $675.00.[3]*

As a follow-up, reports from the mission were distributed to the families. In this way they saw how their God used their money. They could praise God for what He was doing and pray for His blessing on the Bibles in Russia.

A similar project that is a bit less complicated for a church to do is the "Love Loaf" project by World Vision. Over 500,000 households have participated in this creative and worthwhile project. Here's how it works. World Vision will send you or your church as many plastic "Love Loaf" banks as you need. The loaves are then filled with coins by families in their homes. On "Love Loaf-Breaking Sunday" families break the banks and the money is counted. Forty percent is sent to World Vision for their mission outreach. The remainder can be used for mission projects your church supports. (For more information on the "Love Loaf" project write to World Vision, 919 W. Huntington Drive, Monrovia, CA 91016.)

Through World Vision, families can also "adopt" children from other countries. World Vision has pictures of children from many different countries. The family picks the child they would like to support. Each month the family sends a reasonable amount to World Vision for the support of the child. The family gets correspondence from the child. The family can also send suitable gifts and write letters. Children become very enthused about missions when they can see their money helping another child.

You can also encourage families in your church to adopt a missionary family. Compile a list of missionaries from which your church families can choose.

Our own family adopted a missionary family three years ago. We write regularly, pray for them, and send them helps to build their family. We send books for the children, *Family Life Today* magazine, and other books on marriage and family. We try to find other items that they cannot get in Brazil. This has been a happy, enriching experience for us and the Bunches, our adopted missionary family.

There are many other mission projects that can be designed for families in your church. Suggest that your missions committee take a session or two to develop missionary projects for families.

## Family Benevolent Fund

I believe that families should give to the local church. Too much designated giving for other projects can weaken the ministry of the local church. But families can set aside certain amounts above that which they would normally give to the church for special projects. The entire family should be encouraged to sacrifice for this fund. Children can earn money or give part of their allowance. Then the family can pray that God will lead them to someone who has a need.

Our family has such a fund and it is exciting for us to see God use this money. Just last week we were able to help the family of a pastor who is temporarily out of work. We have just heard of a lady in our church who must have an expensive electric wheelchair. We are discussing how much money we can give toward this.

Families can save money to give toward specific needs of the church. Most churches can come up with a rather extensive list of items they really need. Why not publish such a list for families and suggest that they select an item to purchase for the church?

## Projects Around the Church

Most churches have jobs families can do together. Sometimes rooms need to be painted. Grounds need to be cared for. Many times there are time-consuming tasks around the church office that can be done by a family team. A "To Do" list complete with a sign-up schedule could be designed for families.

## Older People

Here is a real opportunity for families to serve—think of the many older persons in your church who are living in retirement and rest homes or who are shut in because of illness. These people love to have persons—especially children—visit them. Encourage families in your church to visit a rest home regularly. Some families might want to adopt an older person who does not have a family. The children could bake cookies, make cards, bring flowers and do other things that would say, "You are special and we love you."

The church needs to help families visualize how they can serve in this way. Some have never thought of this kind of ministry. Give names and addresses of seniors, rest homes and retirement homes to interested families. Provide opportunities for families to report on their experiences. Encourage two or three families to form a team and plan times they can visit a rest home together.

## Prison Ministry

Our family sometimes goes to the Oregon Correctional Facility to participate in the Sunday afternoon chapel program. We make ourselves available to talk to the prisoners that come to the service. In many ways, just our presence encourages the prisoners. Check out the prisons in your area and see if your church families can be of service. There is also a great need for Christian families to sponsor prisoners when they are released from prison.

## Encouragement

Any family can have a ministry of encouraging

others. There is not a person in the church that can't benefit from a little dose of encouragement at times. Phone calls of appreciation to the church leaders can be made. Encouraging notes can be sent. For example, a family could use one family night a month to write encouraging appreciation notes to persons in the church.

## Example

Maybe the most important ministry in which all families can be involved is the ministry of setting an example for others. As a representative of Jesus Christ, the family, by their conduct, can help others see the love of God (see Col. 3:17).

## Families Can Participate in Worship Services

Recently we had a missionary from Mexico in our adult Sunday School class. One of the slides he showed was of a Mexican family singing together in a worship service. I was immediately a little shocked and began to wonder why. Why, I thought, should it look strange for a family to sing a special number in a worship service. A friend sitting nearby had the same reaction as myself. "Why can't we have our families occasionally provide special music?" she asked. "I think it would be really neat."

As a result of that conversation, this year we are scheduling several evening services that will be planned and conducted by teams of three families. There is a lot of enthusiasm and we are sure that this will be a positive step toward equipping families to serve together in the church.

## You Can Start Now

- Use the Scriptures and concepts given in chapter 1

"A Biblical Base for Family Ministry" as study material for an elective Sunday School class.

• Use the material mentioned above along with the ideas in this chapter for a series of evening services titled "Your Family's Opportunities to Serve Jesus." At the end of the series ask families for a commitment to a specific project.

• Have a group of interested persons in your church read this chapter and lay plans to equip families to serve others. (This is a good assignment for a family life committee.)

• Have a "Serving Others" bulletin board. On the bulletin board show names of families and their service projects. Reports and pictures of how these families are serving will motivate other families to serve.

• Note: For additional information on the resources mentioned in this chapter, see "Resources for Equipping Families to Minister to Others" following "Reflect and Respond."

**Reflect and Respond**
1. Do you feel that the 20-80 syndrome exists in your church (20 percent of the people doing 80 percent of the work)? What are some specific examples that cause you to feel this is so?

2. On a scale of 1-10 how would you rank your church families' hospitality to other families in the church? in the community?

3. The author states that families can be the greatest potential for ministry the church has ever seen. How do you feel about that statement?

4. Out of the many ideas in this chapter, list five that you want to encourage families in your church to put into action. Make specific plans for how and when.

5. Is your family involved in a ministry that is a model for other families? How about the families of other leaders in your church?

**Notes**

1. Edith Schaeffer, *What Is a Family?* (Old Tappan: Fleming H. Revell Company, 1975), p. 211
2. Karen B. Mains, *Open Heart—Open Home* (Elgin: David C. Cook Publishing Company, 1976), p. 19.
3. Lud Golz, "How to Get Church Families Involved in Missions," *Moody Monthly* (October, 1977), p. 135.

# Bibliography

**Resources for Building a Personal
Relationship with God**

Biehl, Bobb and Hagelganz, James W. *Praying—How to Start and Keep Going*. Glendale, CA: Regal Books, 1976.

Hendricks, Howard. *Heaven Help the Home!* Wheaton: Victor Books, 1973.

MacDonald, Hope. *Discovering How to Pray*. Grand Rapids: Zondervan Publishing House, 1976.

Miller, Chuck. *Now That I'm a Christian*, Volumes 1,2. Glendale, CA: Regal Books, 1976.

Wollen, Albert J. *Miracle of Group Bible Study*. Glendale, CA: Regal Books, 1976.

*Your Life in Christ*, Book 1. "Design for Discipleship Series," Colorado Springs: Navpress. From the Navigators, Box 1657, Colorado Springs, CO 80901

*The 2:7 Series*. Colorado Springs: Navpress.

*Family Life Today* magazine published monthly by

Gospel Light Publications, 110 W. Broadway, Glendale, CA 91204. Especially see the "Family Time" section.

## Resources for Strengthening Husband-Wife Relationships

Augsburger, David. *Caring Enough to Confront.* Glendale, CA: Regal Books, 1973.

Augsburger, David. *Cherishable: Love and Marriage.* Scottdale, PA: Herald Press, 1971. Tapes to use with the book are available.

Christenson, Larry and Nordis. *The Christian Couple.* Minneapolis: Bethany Fellowship, Inc., 1977.

Clinebell, Howard Jr. *Basic Types of Pastoral Counseling.* Nashville: Abingdon Press, 1966.

Collins, Gary, ed. *How to Be a People Helper.* Santa Ana, CA: Vision House Publishers, 1976. Tapes to use with the book are available.

Dobson, James. *What Wives Wish Their Husbands Knew About Women.* Wheaton: Tyndale House Publishers, 1976.

Foster, Timothy. *Dare to Lead.* Glendale CA: Regal Books, 1977.

Johnson, James L. *What Every Woman Should Know About a Man.* Grand Rapids: Zondervan Publishing House, 1977.

Landorf, Joyce. *Tough and Tender.* Old Tappan: Fleming H. Revell, 1977.

Louthan, Sheldon and Martin, Grant. *Family Ministries in Your Church.* Glendale, CA: Regal Books, 1977.

Merrill, Dean. *The Husband Book.* Elgin: David C. Cook, 1977.

Minirth, Frank B. *Christian Psychiatry.* Old Tappan: Fleming H. Revell, 1977.

Morrow, Fr. Tom and Coleman, Lyman. *Evenings for*

*Couples.* Scottdale, PA: Serendipity House, 1976. A seminar or workshop resource.

Petersen, J. Allan. *Two Become One.* Wheaton: Tyndale House Publishers, 1973.

Rickerson, Wayne E. *Getting Your Family Together.* Glendale, CA: Regal Books, 1977.

Wright, H. Norman. *Communication: Key to Your Marriage.* Glendale, CA: Regal Books, 1976.

Wright, H. Norman. *Communication and Conflict Resolution in Marriage.* Elgin: David C. Cook, 1977. A multimedia kit.

Wright, H. Norman. *Premarital Counseling.* Chicago: Moody Press, 1977.

Wright, H. Norman. *The Christian Faces ... Emotions, Marriage and Family Relationships.* Denver: Christian Marriage Enrichment, 1975. See the seminar resource "The Growing Marriage," p. 85. Mr. Wright conducts Christian marriage enrichment seminars to train participants in the practical skills necessary to lead marriage enrichment weekends and classes. For additional seminar information write to Christian Marriage Enrichment, 1070 Detroit Street, Denver, Colorado 80206.

## Resources for Encouraging Healthy Family Relationships

### I. Parent-Child Relationships

*A. Discipline*

Brandt, Henry R. and Dowdy, Homer E. *Building a Christian Home.* Wheaton: Victor Books, 1960.

Dobson, James. *Dare to Discipline.* Wheaton: Tyndale House Publishers, 1970.

Dobson, James. *Preparing for Adolescence.* Costa Mesa, CA: One Way Library, 1973. Six tapes that speak to teenage problems.

Mow, Anna B. *Your Child.* Grand Rapids: Zondervan Publishing House, 1972.

Narramore, Bruce. *Help, I'm a Parent!* Grand Rapids: Zondervan Publishing House, 1975. The study guide, *A Guide to Child Rearing*, is available for use with this book.

Wakefield, Norm. *You Can Have a Happier Family.* Glendale, CA: Regal Books, 1977. Especially see chapters 2,3.

### B. Self-Esteem

Briggs, Dorothy Corkille. *Your Child's Self-Esteem.* New York: Doubleday & Company, 1970.

Dobson, James. *Hide or Seek.* Old Tappan: Fleming H. Revell Company, 1974.

Wakefield, Norman. *Building Self-Esteem in the Family.* Elgin: David C. Cook, 1977. A multimedia kit.

## II. Family Unity

Hunt, Gladys. *Building Family Unity.* Elgin: David C. Cook, 1977. A multimedia kit.

Hunt, Gladys. *Honey for a Child's Heart.* Grand Rapids: Zondervan Publishing House, 1970.

Rickerson, Wayne E. *Getting Your Family Together.* Glendale, CA: Regal Books, 1977.

Rickerson, Wayne E. *Good Times for Your Family.* Glendale, CA: Regal Books, 1976.

Schaeffer, Edith. *What Is a Family?* Old Tappan: Fleming H. Revell, 1975.

Shedd, Charlie. *Fun Family Forum.* Waco: Word, Inc., 1975. Twelve tapes on different aspects of family living.

Wakefield, Norman. *Building Self-Esteem in the Family.* Elgin: David C. Cook, 1977.

Wakefield, Norman. *You Can Have a Happier Family.* Glendale, CA: Regal Books, 1977.

### III. Recreation

Hendricks, Howard. *Heaven Help the Home!* Wheaton: Victor Books, 1973.

Jacobson, Marion Leach. *How to Keep Your Family Together and Still Have Fun.* Grand Rapids: Zondervan Publishing House, 1969.

Musselman, Virginia. *Making Family Get-Togethers Click.* Harrisburg: Stackpole Books, 1968.

Self, Margaret. *Now What Can We Do?* Glendale, CA: Regal Books, 1977.

Walker, Georgiana. *The Celebration Book.* Glendale, CA: Regal Books, 1977.

### IV. Communication

Augsburger, David. *Caring Enough to Confront.* Glendale, CA: Regal Books, 1974.

Johnson, Rex. *Communication: Key to Your Parents.* Glendale, CA: Regal Books, 1978.

Shedd, Charlie. *Promises to Peter.* Waco: Word, Inc., 1970.

Skoglund, Elizabeth. *Can I Talk to You?* Glendale, CA: Regal Books, 1977.

Swindoll, Charles. *You and Your Child.* Nashville: Thomas Nelson, Inc., 1977.

Wahlroos, Sven. *Family Communication.* New York: Macmillan Publishing Company, Inc., 1974.

Wright, H. Norman. *An Answer to Family Communication.* Irvine, CA: Harvest House Publications, Inc., 1977.

Wright, H. Norman. *Parent-Teen Relationships.* Tapes available from: H.N. Wright, P.O. Box 16279, Irvine, CA 92714.

### V. Single Adults

Andrews, Gini. *Your Half of the Apple.* Grand Rapids: Zondervan Publishing House, 1972.

Bel Geddes, Joan. *How to Parent Alone: A Guide for*

*Single Parents.* Somers, CT: Seabury Press, Inc., 1974.

Jepson, Sarah. *Solo.* Carol Stream, IL: Creation House, Inc., 1970.

McGinnis, Marilyn. *Single.* Old Tappen: Fleming H. Revell Company, 1974.

Payne, Dorothy. *Women Without Men.* New York: United Church Press, 1969.

Potts, Nancy. *Beginning Again: The Challenge of the Formerly Married.* Elgin: David C. Cook, 1977. A multimedia kit.

*Solo* magazine published bimonthly by the Positive Christian Singles of Garden Grove Community Church, 12141 Lewis Street, Garden Grove, CA 92640. $8.00 per year.

Sroka, Barbara. *Building a Single Identity.* Elgin: David C. Cook, 1977. A multimedia kit.

Start, Clarissa. *On Becoming a Widow.* St. Louis: Concordia Publishing House, 1968.

Wiebe, Katie F. *Alone, a Widow's Search for Joy.* Wheaton: Tyndale House Publishers, Inc., 1976.

Organization: *One-Parent Families,* headed by Dr. Charles E. Smith, a marriage, child and family counselor. Information may be obtained by writing to One-Parent Families, 16255 Ventura Blvd., Encino, CA 91426.

## VI. Retirement and Senior Years

Cooper, John C. and Wahlberg, Rachel Conrad. *Your Exciting Middle Years.* Waco: Word, Inc., 1976.

Dye, Harold E. *No Rocking Chair for Me!* Nashville: Broadman Press, 1977.

Otte, Elmer. *Welcome Retirement.* St. Louis: Concordia Publishing House, 1974.

Peter, James A. and Payne, Barbara. *Love in the Later Years.* New York: Association Press, 1975.

Segler, Franklin M. *Alive! and Past 60.* Nashville: Broadman Press, 1977.

Tengbom, Mildred. *The Bonus Years.* Minneapolis: Augsburg Publishing House, 1975.

Vandenburgh, Mildred. *Fill Your Days with Life.* Glendale, CA: Regal Books, 1975.

## Resources for Enabling Parents to Teach Christian Values

Anson, Elva. *How to Keep the Family That Prays Together from Falling Apart.* Chicago: Moody Press, 1975.

Bock, Lois and Working, Miji. *Happiness Is a Family Time Together.* Old Tappan, Fleming H. Revell Company, 1975.

Bock, Lois, and Working, Miji. *Happiness Is a Family Walk with God.* Old Tappan: Fleming H. Revell Company, 1977.

Collins, Gary R., ed. *Facing the Future: Church and Family Together.* Waco: Word, Inc., 1976.

Mow, Anna B. *Your Child.* Grand Rapids: Zondervan Publishing House, 1972.

Narramore, Bruce. *An Ounce of Prevention.* Grand Rapids: Zondervan Publishing House, 1973.

Rickerson, Wayne E. *Getting Your Family Together.* Glendale, CA: Regal Books, 1977.

Rickerson, Wayne E. *Good Times for Your Family.* Glendale, CA: Regal Books, 1976.

Wakefield, Norman. *You Can Have a Happier Family.* Glendale, CA: Regal Books, 1977.

*Family Life Today* magazine, published monthly by Gospel Light Publications, 110 W. Broadway, Glendale, CA 91204. $8.00 per year.

**Seminars:**

a. *Creative Home Teaching Seminars.* For information

143

write to Wayne E. Rickerson, 13600 SW Allen Blvd., Beaverton, Oregon 97005.

b. *Sunday School Plus.* For information write to Sunday School Plus, 1411 North Sixth St., Phoenix, Arizona 85002.

## Resources for Equipping Families to Minister to Others

Collins, Gary. *Facing the Future: Church and Family Together.* Waco: Word, Inc., 1976.

Deen, Edith. *Family Living in the Bible.* Moonachie, NJ: Pyramid Publications, 1969.

Getz, Gene. *The Measure of a Family.* Glendale, CA: Regal Books, 1973.

Hendricks, Howard. *Heaven Help the Home!* Wheaton: Victor Books, 1973.

Louthan, Sheldon, and Martin, Grant. *Family Ministries in Your Church.* Glendale, CA: Regal Books, 1977.

Mains, Karen B. *Open Heart—Open Home.* Elgin: David C. Cook Publishing Company, 1976.